# The British Empire 1870–1914

**Martin Roberts**

LONGMAN

First published 1995

ISBN 0 582 082579

Set in 11/15pt Bodoni (Lasercomp)
Printed in Hong Kong
SWT/01

The publishers policy is to use paper
manufactured from sustainable forests

Designed and illustrated
by Michael Harris

We are grateful to the following for
permission to reproduce copyright
photographs:

Africana Museum, Johannesburg, page 37;
Royal Geographical Society, London/
Bridgeman Art Library, London, page 8; by
permission of the British Library/Oriental
and India Office Collections, pages 16
(Add.Or. 3853), 18 (Add.Or 1260), 20, 22
(below), 62 (above and below); by
permission of the Syndics of Cambridge
University Library/Royal Commonwealth
Society Collection, pages 24 (right), 63, 76;
Church Missionary Society, page 59; print
taken from 'A Concise History of the British
Empire', Thames and Hudson, (source
unknown), page 68; De Beers Consolidated
Mines, page 42; Robert Harding Picture
Library, page 80; Hulton Deutsch Collection
Limited, pages 12, 31, 32, 35, 65, 66, 78
(below); The Illustrated London News
Picture Library, pages 6, 7, 41, 57, 73;
Imperial War Museum, London, page 78
(above); The Mansell Collection Limited,
pages 26, 27, 28, 30 (left and right), 33
(above and below), 43, 46 (below), 52, 58, 64,
67, 74; The Mayibuye Centre, South Africa,
page 48; from 'Moonshine', 5 March 1898,
page 56; courtesy of the Director, National
Army Museum, London, page 19 (centre
left); National Cultural History Museum,
South Africa, page 46 (above); by Courtesy
of the National Portrait Gallery, London,
pages 19 (above right), 22 (centre), 24 (left);
by permission of Dr. Chris Pinney, 60;
copyprint after photograph in Nehru
Memorial Museum and Library, New Delhi,
page 22 (above); Picturepoint-London, page
70; Popperfoto, pages 5, 71, 75; Punch, page
19 (below right); South African Library,
pages 38, 39, 40, 44; Tony Stone Images,
page 15; Topham Picture Source, page 34;
Weidenfeld Archives, page 72.

Cover: Topham Picture Source

Picture Research by Sandie Huskinson-
Rolfe (PHOTOSEEKERS)

# Contents

# Introduction

Empires arise when one country or ruler (sometimes called an emperor or empress) obtains power over other countries. Trade and religion often play a part in empire building, but war and conquest are seldom far behind.

Turn back the clock 300 years. In 1700, there were three great empires in the world: the Mughal Empire of India, the Manchu Empire of China and the Ottoman Empire ruled by the Sultan of Turkey. Britain played only a minor role on the world stage. British naval strength was growing, but the Dutch remained the world's greatest sea power.

The world looked quite different 150 years later. By 1850, the Mughal Empire was virtually dead, and the Ottoman and Manchu Empires were very weak. It was the European nations who were advancing in industrial and technological might. Soon they would use this strength to conquer much of the

**1** **The world in 1700.**

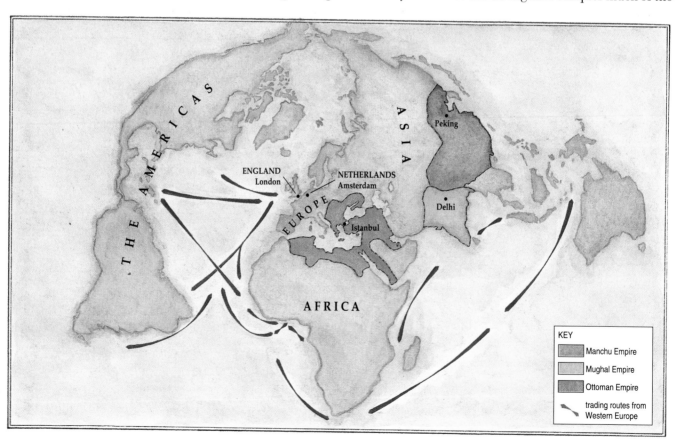

KEY

Manchu Empire

Mughal Empire

Ottoman Empire

trading routes from Western Europe

**2** **The entrance to Government House, Calcutta.**

world. Britain, the most advanced industrial nation with the most powerful navy, was about to create the largest empire the world has ever seen.

The archway shown in the photograph (source 2) tells us much about the confidence of Britain's rulers at that time. The lion, representing Britain, stands on top of the main entrance to Government House in Calcutta, from where Britain ruled India. Beneath the lion's paw is the globe. The message is simple: the world lies at Britain's feet.

Turn the clock forward another 150 years, to the present. Today, there is one military superpower, the USA, and two economic superpowers, the USA and Japan. The area showing the most rapid economic advance is the Far East.

The nations of Europe, though industrially and technologically advanced, have lost their empires. A number of countries have joined together to form the European Community (EC). Britain's world role has shrunk. It is just one of the comparatively well-off members of the EC. Britannia does not rule the waves (nor the skies). Of the British Empire, only a few ports and islands are left.

The aim of this book is to describe the years 1870–1914, when the British Empire grew fastest, and the effects of this growth both on Britain and on the conquered peoples of the Empire. It is an extraordinary and controversial story, since the Empire changed the lives of millions of people – for better and for worse. Not surprisingly, it was generally the British who saw its good points, though there were many British critics of the Empire. The rest of the world had little difficulty finding the bad ones.

# 1 The origins and growth of Empire

**1** Queen Victoria and the Empire she reigned over for so long are celebrated on the front cover of the *Illustrated London News*, 26 June 1897. The Diamond Jubilee was the subject of a special supplement.

## The Diamond Jubilee, 1897

Queen Victoria's Diamond Jubilee was a national celebration to mark the fact that she had ruled Great Britain for sixty years. On 22 June 1897 the Queen attended a service at St Paul's Cathedral to give thanks for the years of her reign, which had been amongst the most successful in British history.

If the much-loved queen was the inspiration for the Jubilee, her worldwide empire was its central theme. Before she left for St Paul's, Victoria tapped out in morse code a message to her hundreds of millions of subjects. By means of the electric telegraph, the short and simple greeting from the Queen Empress circled the globe in a few minutes. 'From my heart I thank my people. May God bless them.'

Fifty thousand troops took part in the great processions through the streets of London, including cavalry from Australia, camel riders from India, Dyak from North Borneo and Maori from New Zealand. In the opinion of the *Daily Mail*:

**2** *The soldiers are all so smart and straight and strong, every man such a splendid specimen and testimony to* [proof of] *the GREATNESS OF THE BRITISH RACE that there was not an Imperialist* [supporter of the Empire] *in the crowd who did not from the sight of them gain a new view of the glory of the British Empire.*

The *Daily Mail* Special Jubilee Issue, June 1897

# The British Empire before 1870

By 1870, the British Empire was certainly mighty (see source 7). It was the largest in human history, stretching over 11 million square miles, a fifth of all the land in the world. In the countries ruled by Britain 372 million people were living, a quarter of the world's population. The proud boast that the sun never set on the British Empire was literally true, for Britain had colonies and outposts in the most remote parts of every continent.

The sea and British sea power linked the Empire together. As you can see in source 6, for centuries British ships had been exploring the oceans in search of new trade and wealth. Where trade was good, British merchants set up trading posts. Where the climate and land were suitable (and the original inhabitants few or weak), British settlers, mainly farmers at first, established colonies. Wherever they raised the British flag, traders and settlers alike could usually depend on the largest navy in the world to defend them.

The British Empire of the sixteenth and seventeenth centuries had grown out of the search for goods to trade, like silk or precious metals in India and the Far East, and lands to settle, in America and Asia. Meanwhile, other European countries – especially Portugal, Spain, the Netherlands and France – were establishing rival empires. By the end of the seventeenth century, Britain had colonies (foreign land under British control) in North America, the West Indies and India. Together, these colonies made up the British Empire.

3 The British Navy – all 30 miles of it – at the 1897 Spithead Review. An engraving from the *Illustrated London News.*

**4** **Sydney in the mid-nineteenth century, in a painting by Thomas Baines.**

During the eighteenth century, Britain gained control of the world's sea routes by defeating France in a series of wars. Between 1750 and 1830, British colonies grew in number, size and wealth. Canada, Australia, New Zealand and South Africa began to attract settlers. The only serious setback came in 1776, when most of the North American colonies declared their independence, won the war with Britain which followed, and became the United States of America.

In the first half of the nineteenth century, however, neither British governments nor public opinion were enthusiastic supporters of the Empire. Governments worried about its costs. Richard Cobden, a leading Liberal MP, spoke against colonies in Manchester in 1849:

**5** *We are told that we must keep up enormous armaments because we have so many colonies. People tell me I want to abandon our colonies; but I say, do you intend to hold your colonies by the sword, by armies, and ships of war?*

*Speeches by Richard Cobden, MP*, eds J. Bright and J. E. Thorold, 1880

Cobden and others argued for trading as freely as possible (without import and export taxes, called tariffs) with as many countries as possible. This, they said, would be better for Britain than taking on the costs and responsibilities of colonial rule. Britain's industrial and naval strength would suit a 'free trade' policy, and the country's share of world trade would increase.

British governments therefore lessened their hold on the mainly 'settler' colonies like Canada and Australia by giving them self-government. When they sent the navy to interfere in other parts of the world, it was usually part of their campaign against slavery, which had been abolished within the British Empire in 1833. When new colonies were established, they tended to be ports and harbours like Hong Kong (1841) and Singapore (1846), which made Britain's control of the world's trade routes even more secure.

| | |
|---|---|
| 1497 | John Cabot, sailing from Bristol in the service of King Henry VII, reaches North America. |
| 1567 and after | Humphrey Gilbert, Martin Frobisher and John Davis explore north-eastern Canada in search of a passage to the Indies around the north of America. |
| 1577 | Francis Drake sails round the world. |
| 1600 | The East India Company is set up to develop trade with India and the Far East. |
| 1606–40 | Colonies are started in North America, e.g., Virginia. In the West Indies, colonies produce tobacco and sugar with slave labour from Africa. The slave trade is very profitable in the eighteenth century. |
| 1756–63 | Britain defeats its rival, France, in the Seven Years' War. Britain takes control of Canada and parts of India. |
| 1770 | James Cook reaches Australasia. |
| 1777–81 | War of American Independence. The 13 American colonies fight their way out of the British Empire. |
| 1780s | First convict settlements in Australia. |
| 1793–1815 | Wars against France. Battle of Trafalgar, 1805, gives British navy control of the world's oceans. |
| 1806 | British win control of Cape Town in South Africa. |
| Early 1800s | British rule spreads in India, Australia, New Zealand and South Africa. |
| 1869 | Suez Canal is opened, linking the Mediterranean and the Indian Ocean. |
| 1870–1914 | Britain and other European nations scramble for colonies, mainly in Africa but also in Asia and in the Pacific. |

**6** The British Empire, 1497–1914.

1 Explain the phrase, 'the Empire upon which the sun never sets'.
2 Explain the difference between 'settlers' and 'traders'.
3 Name three areas of the world attractive to British settlers, and one which broke away from the Empire.
4 Why was Richard Cobden (in source 5) against more colonies?
5 In what way did the British Empire expand between 1815 and 1850?

# The growth of the British Empire, 1870–1914

In the second half of the nineteenth century, attitudes to the Empire changed. Politicians and the British people began to favour the colonies. This was mainly because the world was changing, and other European nations seemed to threaten Britain's worldwide power.

In 1869 the Suez Canal opened up an important new sea route from Europe to India. Designed by Ferdinand de Lesseps, a Frenchman, and paid for by French as well as British money, it was not under British control. Other European countries, notably France, Belgium and Germany, had become interested in empire building. Other countries, such as Germany and the USA, were challenging Britain's economic lead.

In the last quarter of the nineteenth century, the nations of Europe were competing feverishly for colonies, mainly in Africa, but also in Asia and the Pacific. They were greedy for land, trade and raw materials like gold and rubber. Each country wanted to keep ahead of its rivals. By 1914 virtually all of Africa, the Pacific islands, and huge areas of Asia were ruled by Europeans.

**7** **The British Empire in 1870.**

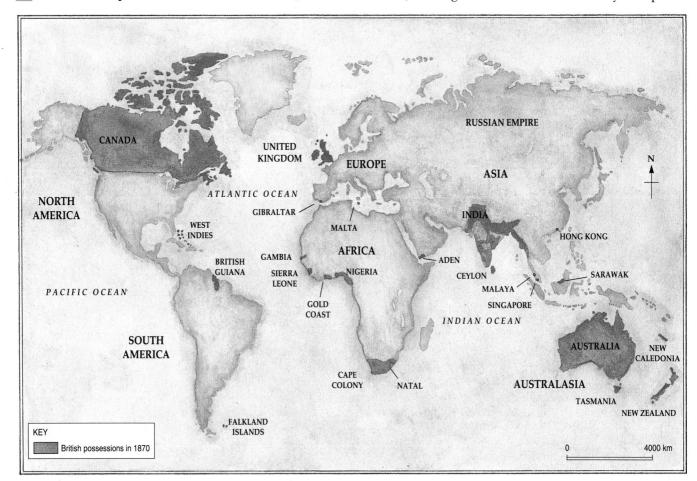

KEY
British possessions in 1870

0          4000 km

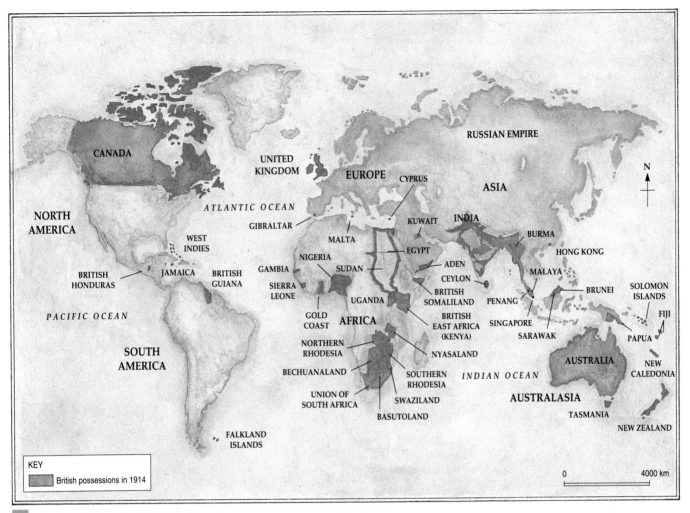

**8** The British Empire in 1914.

## The Suez Canal and the scramble for Africa, 1875–1902

The scramble for Africa began in Egypt. Disraeli saw the Suez Canal, which ran through Egypt, as the key to India. It was the vital link in the sea route along which passed much of the profitable Indian trade, and the ships and troops which guarded that trade.

Disraeli decided to take an increasing interest in Egyptian affairs. In 1875, he bought from the bankrupt ruler of Egypt his shares in the Suez Canal company (see source 9), and Britain and France took joint control of Egyptian finances. By 1882 Britain was in effective control of Egypt (see Chapter 3), while France was looking for gains elsewhere in north and west Africa to balance Britain's success in Egypt.

The huge imperial ambitions of Leopold II, King of Belgium, set the pace of the scramble for Africa. In 1876 he set up the International African Association and sent the explorer H. M. Stanley to explore the Congo River region. In less than ten years, Leopold II had gained the so-called Congo Free State. Britain, France, Germany, Portugal and Italy all followed his example.

12

**9** This *Punch* cartoon shows Disraeli, accompanied by the British lion, buying the Suez canal shares for Queen Victoria.

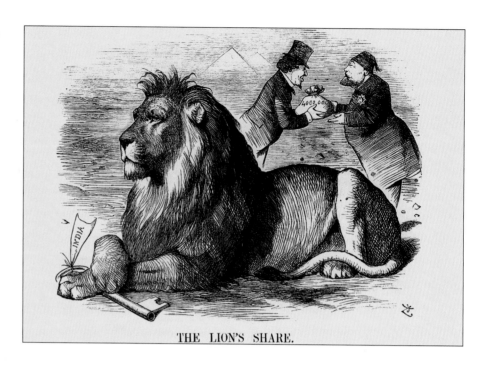

THE LION'S SHARE.

You can see the result of this 'scramble' in source 8. Britain definitely got the lion's share.

## The Empire spreads eastwards

In Asia there was a similar scramble for the Pacific islands and for the ports along the China coast. The huge population of China was a very attractive market for Euopean goods. The strength of the navy made sure that Britain, once again, got what the empire builders wanted. Meanwhile, north-west India looked open to attack from Russia, which also had imperial ambitions. To strengthen the borders, the British brought Afghanistan and parts of Persia under their 'influence'. This meant having more political and economic say in those parts than any other foreign country, without actually taking control.

**1 Unjumble the following:**

| | | |
|---|---|---|
| Belgium | The Suez canal | The frontiers of India |
| France | Afghanistan | The sea route to India |
| Russia | The Congo | The scramble for Africa |

**2** Describe what the *Punch* cartoon (source 9) actually shows. Then explain its political message.

# The popularity of empire building

By the 1890s, both politicians and the public wanted to add more countries to the Empire. From 1895 to 1900, the Colonial Secretary was Joseph Chamberlain, whose strong support for imperialist policies was well known. Soon after his appointment he spoke at the recently opened Imperial Institute in London:

**10** *I believe in the British Empire (cheers), and . . . I believe in the British race. (Cheers.) I believe that the British race is the greatest of the governing races that the world has ever seen. (Cheers.) I say that not as an empty boast, but as proved by the success which we have had in administering vast dominions which are connected with these small islands.*

*The Times*, 12 November 1895

The public did not worry about the risk of war as a result of empire building. As a leading Liberal politician, Sir Edward Grey, remembered in 1906:

**11** *Before the Boer War* [in South Africa, 1899–1902] *we were spoiling for a fight. We were ready to fight France about Siam . . . and Russia about anything. Any government here, during the last ten years of the last century, could have had war by lifting a finger. The people would have shouted for it. They had a craving for excitement, and a rush of blood to the head.*

Sir Edward Grey in conversation in 1906, quoted by Bernard Porter, *The Lion's Share*, 1984

At the end of the nineteenth century, the British Empire was at its strongest and at the height of its popularity with the British people. It had grown steadily for three hundred years and then with astonishing speed during the last twenty-five. The chapters which follow are case studies of India, Egypt and South Africa, which show how British rule took hold in these key areas of the world, and the consequences both for Britain and for the indigenous people of those countries.

# Review and Assessment

**1** Compare the two maps, sources 7 and 8 (pages 10–11).

**a** Where, in 1870, were Britain's most important possessions (i) in Africa and (ii) in Asia?

**b** In which continent did Britain make the greatest gains between 1870 and 1914? Name three colonies gained in these years.

**c** How did the building of the Suez Canal change the focus of British thinking about the Empire?

**2** Study this table of British exports.

|  | Average per year (in millions of £) | | | |
|---|---|---|---|---|
|  | Europe | USA/Canada | Africa | Asia |
| 1870–9 | 87.1 | 33.4 | 6.9 | 37.4 |
| 1900–9 | 119 | 36.1 | 25.8 | 71.0 |
| % increase 1870–1909 | 37 | 8 | 274 | 90 |

**1** Exports to different parts of the world, 1870–1909

**a** Draw bar charts of these figures (you do not need to show the percentages). Then answer these questions:

**b** Which areas were Britain's largest and second-largest export markets in the 1870s, and which in the 1900s?

**c** In which area had British trade expanded fastest by 1900, and in which area had it expanded least?

**d** What does source 1 tell you about the importance of the expansion of the British Empire in Africa and Asia as far as British exports were concerned?

# 2 India under the Raj

The British connection with India began in the sixteenth century, when the East India Company was set up to buy precious stones and cloth. By the nineteenth century, the company represented and protected all British interests in India. The industrial revolution brought a change in the pattern of trade. It led to cloth being *exported* by Britain, along with other factory-made goods (see below). Gradually, Britain took over political control of the country from the local rulers. The Raj is the name given to the period of British rule in India, particularly the years from 1858 to 1914.

## The Mughal Empire

In the sixteenth and seventeenth centuries the subcontinent of India was made up of a number of separate states, many of them ruled by the Mughal emperors. They were fine warriors and, though themselves Muslims, treated their Hindu subjects tolerantly. They provided good government and built many splendid buildings, including the Taj Mahal.

Source 1 shows the Taj Mahal, built in white marble between 1632 and 1652 in memory of Shahjahan's much-loved wife, Mumtaz, who died in childbirth.

**1** The Taj Mahal.

**2** Shahjahan at his *durbar*, or ceremonial gathering. The scene was painted by a Mughal artist in about 1650.

In source 2 (top centre, holding a jewel, with a halo round his head), you can see the Mughal Emperor Shahjahan.

**1  What evidence is there in sources 1 and 2 that the Mughals were powerful and civilised rulers?**

# The East India Company

The British found that trading with India was very profitable. As the Mughal Empire grew weaker in the eighteenth century, the East India Company made alliances with local Indian princes to increase its trade at the expense of the French. Then, supported by the British government, the Company turned on the Indian princes and won control of much of the Indian subcontinent (see source 3). The Mughal emperors maintained their court in Delhi until 1858, but long before that they had lost all their former power.

India was the 'jewel in the crown' of the British Empire for two main reasons. First, it was good for trade. In the seventeenth and eighteenth centuries, the British bought goods manufactured in India, like silk and cloth, and sold them in Europe and in Asia. Increasingly, in the nineteenth century, they sold British manufactured goods to the large Indian market, particularly cheap cottons from Lancashire. By 1900, 45 per cent of all British cotton exports went to India.

2 Describe the main stages by which the British gained control of the trade and land of India.

3 What were the two main reasons why India was described as the jewel in the crown of the British Empire?

4 How did British trade with India change between the seventeenth century and the nineteenth century?

3 India in 1857, showing the Mughal Empire at its greatest extent, and the extent of British rule.

KEY
- territory under British rule in 1805
- territory brought under British control between 1805 and 1856
- Mughal Empire

**4** Gurkha chiefs and soldiers in 1830. These tough soldiers from the mountains of northern India manned some of the best-known regiments in the British army in the nineteenth and twentieth centuries. They fought for Britain in the First and Second World Wars.

The second reason was the Indian army, 300,000 strong, of whom only about 45,000 were British. This army was the largest fighting force outside Europe. It could be moved anywhere in the world by the British navy and fought in many imperial wars. Its costs were paid for entirely out of Indian taxes, not British ones.

Until 1858, the East India Company was still in charge of India – in partnership with the British government, which appointed the Governor-General and the senior army officers. Company officials collected taxes and maintained law and order. The Company traded not only in British and Indian goods, but in products from other parts of Asia, too. Shipping Indian opium to China and returning with Chinese tea was particularly profitable.

1 What triggered off the Indian Mutiny and Rebellion in 1857?

2 What other reasons were there for it?

3 Explain the cartoon, 'Justice', source 8.

4 Source 8 is a British cartoon, published in a British magazine. What caption might an Indian have given it?

# The Indian Mutiny and Rebellion, 1857–8

In 1857, British rule was severely shaken by an Indian rising. The British called it 'the Indian Mutiny' since it began with the refusal of Indian soldiers to obey the orders of their British officers. Indian historians prefer to describe it as the Great Rebellion since in their view it was a widespread rebellion against the British, and not an army mutiny alone.

The rebellion began at the important army base of Meerut, near Delhi, when Indian soldiers turned on their officers because they had ordered them to do something intolerable on religious grounds to both Muslims and Hindus. Muslims consider pork to be 'unclean' and the cow is a sacred animal to Hindus. The British had ordered the soldiers to handle cartridges coated with a mixture of pork and beef fat! This was typical of British rule at that time. It had little respect for Indian customs, believing them to be backward and foolish. The government had made many other changes without consulting Indian opinion. Changes affecting land-holding and religion upset the Indians most.

A rebel pamphlet of 1857 declared that:

5 *It is well-known that in these days all the English have entertained these evil designs* [have these evil plans] – *first to destroy the religion of the whole Hindustani army and to make the people by compulsion Christians.*

Quoted by P. C. Joshi, *Rebellion 1857: A Symposium*, 1957

During the revolt there were barbaric cruelties on both sides. At Cawnpore, Indian rebels stabbed to death more than 200 British women and children, and threw their bodies down a well. British regiments destroyed whole villages and took no prisoners, slaughtering on the spot anyone suspected of being a rebel. Though the risings were widespread, they were patchy and disunited. After 14 months the British were once more in control.

7 **The Rani of Jhansi. The Rani, whose lands the British had taken from her when her husband died, fought against the British in 1857 and was killed in action. She became a heroine of Indian nationalism in the late nineteenth century. This portrait was painted in about 1890.**

6 **Miss Wheeler defending herself against the sepoys at Cawnpore.**

Back in Britain, a shocked public cried out for vengeance. In India, the soldiers who were found guilty of mutiny were publicly bound to the muzzles of cannons and blown to bits.

Neither side forgot these events. The British, who were always a tiny minority in India, grew less ready to mix with Indians and came down hard on any sign of disorder or anti-British feeling. For their part, the Indians remembered the heroes and heroines of the rebellion and the cruelty of the British in crushing it.

JUSTICE.

8 **'Justice', a cartoon from *Punch*, 12 September 1857.**

# British rule in India, 1858–1914

As a result of the Indian Mutiny and Rebellion, the British government took direct control of India. It sent the last Mughal emperor into exile and abolished the East India Company. It appointed a Viceroy as head of government, advised by a small council. Government orders were carried out by some 2,000 British civil servants. Many of them were district officers or collector-magistrates, whose main tasks were to see that taxes were collected and laws obeyed. (See also Chapter 6, pages 60–2.)

The greatest achievement of the Raj was the building of railways, roads, irrigation systems and other public works (see Chapter 7). A striking example is the very decorative railway station in Bombay, typical of Victorian architecture. These public works helped Indian agriculture and industry in many ways. Britain gained as well, by controlling the Indian economy in its own interest.

At home, Britain prided itself on how free the British people were, on its elected parliament and, from the 1860s, on its readiness to extend the right to vote to more and more of its citizens. In India, however, Britain's attitude was quite different.

**9  Victoria railway station, Bombay, painted in 1878.**

In the 1830s, the famous historian and liberal politician, T. B. Macaulay, had looked forward to the day when India would be self-governing:

**10** *The public mind of India may . . . in some future age, demand European institutions . . . Whenever* [that time] *comes it will be the proudest day in English history.*

Quoted by E. Stokes, *The English Utilitarians and India*, 1959

By the 1880s, partly as a result of the Indian Mutiny and Rebellion, the mood of the British civil servants in India was different. As one of them wrote in the 1880s:

**11** *We cannot foresee the time in which the cessation* [end] *of our rule would not be the signal for universal anarchy and ruin . . . the only hope for India is the long continuance of the benevolent but strong government of Englishmen.*

Sir John Strachey, quoted by E. Stokes, *The English Utilitarians and India*, 1959

# Indian nationalism

Educated Indians quickly saw the glaring difference between Britain, the champion of freedom and of parliamentary government, and Britain, the stern ruler of India unwilling to share any power with its hundreds of millions of subjects.

Members of the urban Indian middle class, a small group in those days, set up the Indian National Congress in 1885. For many years, under the influence of men like the university professor G. K. Ghokale, it was moderate, not revolutionary. It aimed not at independence but at self-government within the British Empire like Canada or Australia. At the second meeting of Congress in 1886, this resolution was passed:

**12** *Self-government is the ordering of nature, the will of Divine Providence . . . But do we govern ourselves? The answer is no . . . We are passing through a period of probation . . . under the auspices of* [watched over by] *one of the most freedom-loving nations of the world. And we claim that the period of probation may now fairly terminate* [come to an end].

Quoted by Annie Besant, *How India Wrought for Freedom*, 1915

**13** G. K. Gokhale, first leader of the Indian National Congress.

**15** B. G. Tilak, a forceful Indian nationalist.

**1** What were the main differences between Gokhale and Tilak as nationalist leaders?

However, many nationalists became impatient with this moderate, peaceful approach. Inspired in part by a strong revival of the Hindu religion, they looked forward not just to self-government but to complete independence. They found an able leader in B. G. Tilak, lawyer and journalist. He was critical of Gokhale's moderate policy towards the British government. As he wrote in his paper, *Kesari*, in 1897:

**14** *In the last 12 years we have been shouting at the Government to hear us. But our shouting has had no more effect . . . than the sound of a gnat . . . We must now give the best possible education to the ignorant villagers . . . and teach them their rights.*

B. G. Tilak, *Kesari*, 12 January 1897

Rather than beg the British for self-government, he wrote fiery articles in his newspapers, appearing to support those nationalists ready to use violence against the Raj. This led to his arrest and imprisonment but failed to silence him. He also made nationalism more attractive to less educated Indians by starting an annual festival in honour of Sivaji, a popular hero who had fought successfully against the British in the seventeenth century.

# Lord Curzon

The Viceroy of India from 1898 to 1905 was a clever English nobleman, Lord Curzon. He was very hard-working but also held a high opinion of his own

**16** Lord and Lady Curzon at a tiger shoot.

abilities. A fellow student at Oxford University summed him up in a rhyme which haunted him for the rest of his career.

**17** *My name is George Nathaniel Curzon,*
*I am a most superior person.*

Quoted by James Morris, *Farewell the Trumpets*, 1978

Curzon refused to take the Indian National Congress seriously. Of it he said:

**18** *The noise comes forth as the voice of India, but when you go to the*
*other end of the funnel, you find that it is nothing of the kind.*

Quoted by Bernard Porter, *The Lion's Share*, 1984

He believed that Congress supporters were only a small minority of discontented middle-class city-dwellers and that the huge majority of the Indian peasantry were loyal to the Empire. They could be kept loyal by fair government and racial tolerance.

Curzon carried out a number of reforms without any regard for Indian opinion. His reform of the city government of Calcutta proved hugely unpopular; so did his division of the province of Bengal. Curzon described the nationalist opposition as 'mere froth', but it was totally serious. Young Bengali nationalists turned to violence and murdered some British officials.

In 1905 a Liberal government came to power in Britain, and with it a new Indian Secretary, John Morley, and a new Viceroy, Lord Minto. Romesh Dutt, a nationalist leader, wrote straight away to Morley:

**19** *They* [Indians] *will not believe that in these days of political progress*
*all over the world, the most Liberal government which England has*
*seen within thirty years will leave India in discontent and despair.*

Quoted by S. A. Wolpert, *Morley and India*, 1967

Morley's aim was to give enough representation to Indians to lessen the discontent without giving so much that it would weaken Britain's power. The so-called Morley-Minto reforms of 1909 placed Indians for the first time on the Viceroy's council and on provincial councils, too. Some of the provincial councillors were elected. The government gave the impression that it was prepared to consult more widely and listen to advice. Consequently, the Morley-Minto reforms gained the support of moderate nationalists like Gokhale. Tilak, however, continued to oppose the moderate line and tried, without success, to win control of the Congress in 1907. More anti-British newspaper articles led the government to impose a six-year prison sentence on Tilak in 1908.

The Morley-Minto reforms temporarily dampened the fires of Indian nationalism but they did not extinguish them. Ten years later they were again burning furiously and could not be put out. It would be 40 years, however, before India was independent.

**20** Shivaji, a seventeenth-century Hindu hero, as he was depicted on an early twentieth-century poster.

**21** The memorial well at Cawnpore, erected by the British in 1864 in memory of the women and children killed in 1857 (see page 19).

**1 Unjumble the following:**

| Curzon | strong nationalist | leader of the Indian National Congress |
|--------|-------------------|---------------------------------------|
| Gokhale | Secretary for India | 1909 Reforms |
| Morley | Viceroy | imprisoned |
| Tilak | moderate nationalist | divided Bengal |

**2 a)** Put source 18 into your own words to make Curzon's meaning clear.

**b)** Which Indian group did he believe to be the most important and how did he intend to keep it loyal?

**3** Why should Romesh Dutt (source 19) believe that in 1905 people in India were discontented and despairing as a result of Curzon's rule?

**4** How much say had Indians in the government of India in 1914?

**5** Shivaji (source 20) was a prince in western India, a successful general greatly respected by English merchants of the East India Company. Why did Indian nationalists choose Shivaji to be one of their special heroes?

**6** What would they have thought of the Cawnpore memorial?

# 3 Egypt and the Sudan

The trading link between Britain and India has lasted four hundred years, and for half that time India was the most important part of the British Empire. In contrast, British rule in Egypt lasted barely forty years and was mainly the result of the scramble for colonies by rival European countries at the end of the nineteenth century.

In 1870 Egypt was part of the Ottoman or Turkish Empire. Its rulers, known as Khedives, owed allegiance to the Turkish Sultan whose capital was

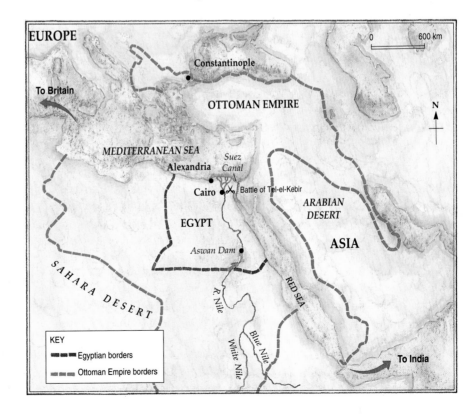

**1** Egypt and the Ottoman Empire in 1879.

**2** Muhammad Ali.

Constantinople. Most Egyptians were Arabs who followed the Muslim religion. Most were also *fellahin*, or peasant farmers, on the fertile banks of the Nile. They used farming methods hundreds, even thousands of years old.

Foreigners from other parts of the Ottoman Empire had been Egypt's Khedives for generations, and a mainly Turkish upper class owned most Egyptian land. Hard work, high taxes and poverty dominated the life of the *fellahin*.

# Muhammad Ali, 1769–1849

Muhammad Ali was an Albanian soldier who campaigned so successfully in Egypt that the Turkish Sultan appointed him as governor there in 1806. He turned out to be an energetic reformer whose aim was to make Egypt richer and less backward by modernising it along European lines.

Muhammad Ali could be cunning and ruthless. For example, he removed some troublesome nobles by inviting them to a banquet where he had them killed. But it is for his achievements that he is remembered. As well as creating a new Egyptian army, he built canals, roads, bridges and new irrigation schemes. This laid the basis for expanding the cultivation of cotton, which later became Egypt's main export. He also encouraged young Egyptians to visit Europe to study the latest developments in science and technology. In the opinion of a modern historian:

> **3** *His achievements were amazing. He put Egypt on the way to modernisation and independence.*

Longman, *The Making of Modern Africa*, Vol. 1, 1986

Muhammad Ali's successsors did not have his abilities. Ismail, who ruled from 1863 to 1879, shared many of his ideas but, unfortunately, was a reckless spender who borrowed heavily to pay for his ambitious schemes. This later gave Britain an opportunity to bring Egypt into the Empire, as we shall see.

1 **Egypt has much the same climate as the Sahara desert. How can anyone live there?**

2 **Who were the *fellahin*? How were they usually treated by the rulers of Egypt?**

3 **Who was, in theory, the supreme ruler of Egypt? What was the title of the actual ruler?**

4 **Why did Muhammad Ali send young Egyptians to Europe?**

5 **What were his main achievements and where did his successors go wrong?**

# The Suez Canal

One large project which Ismail borrowed heavily to pay for was the building of the Suez Canal. The canal quickly aroused Britain's interest in Egypt by becoming the major sea-route from Europe to India. It was designed by a brilliant French engineer, de Lesseps, and constructed mainly by French contractors. The money for it was raised by the Suez Canal Company, which sold shares or 'bonds' to the general public. The bondholders, the majority of whom were French or British, purchased the shares expecting that once the Canal started business they would make money out of its profits. Ismail treated the Suez Canal Company generously. He also bought 40 per cent of its shares, borrowing from British and French banks to do so.

The canal opened in 1869. In the 1870s, 80 per cent of the shipping using it was British. By 1875, Ismail was só deeply in debt that he let it be known that his shares were up for sale. Disraeli, the British Prime Minister, saw the opportunity and pounced. To prevent the canal falling into unfriendly hands, he bought Ismail's shares for £4,000,000. As he explained to the House of Commons:

> **4** *I do not recommend this purchase as a financial investment . . . I recommend it to the country as a political transaction, and one which I believe is calculated to strengthen the Empire.*

Quoted in Longman, *The Making of Modern Africa*, Vol. 1, 1986

Disraeli's great rival, W. E. Gladstone, criticised the purchase. In his opinion, it could only lead to trouble:

> **6** *Our first site in Egypt, be it by larceny* [theft] *or emption* [paying], *will be the almost certain egg of a North African Empire which will grow and grow . . . We may be territorially content but less than ever at our ease.*

Quoted by Sir Philip Magnus, *Gladstone*, 1954

Gladstone had good reason to be worried. The Egyptian egg, laid by Disraeli, hatched in 1882. By then, Gladstone had taken over as Prime Minister and had to decide what to do with a chicken which, as he had predicted, grew and grew.

# The Nationalist Revolt of 1882

Ismail's debts swelled and his hold on Egypt weakened. In the interests of their bondholders, Britain and France forced him to resign in favour of his son Tewfik, and took control of Egypt's finances. This action caused a nationalist revot.

The revolt was led by the popular Colonel Arabi, one of the few *fellahin* to have risen to senior rank in the Egyptian army. His slogan 'Egypt for the

**5** A British transport ship sailing through the canal: a picture from the *Illustrated London News* of 12 July 1882.

6 Where does the Suez canal run from and to?
7 Why was it so important to Britain?
8 Who were Disraeli and Gladstone?
9 In source 4, what reason does Disraeli give for purchasing the Suez Canal shares? In source 6, why is Gladstone unhappy about Britain getting involved in Egypt?

**7** Arabi at the bombardment of Alexandria, as seen by an artist in the *Illustrated London News* of 22 July 1882.

Egyptians' met with general enthusiasm, particularly in Cairo and Alexandria. Arabi forced Tewfik to appoint a nationalist government consisting of an elected council of ministers, with himself as Minister of War.

Arabi made Britain and France uneasy. If he was successful, the bondholders might not get their money and the Suez Canal could be in danger. When, in 1882, rioters killed some Europeans in Alexandria, a joint Anglo-French fleet appeared off the Egyptian coast. The French decided that the situation did not require military action and sailed away, but the British bombarded Alexandria and then landed a force which destroyed Arabi's army in a surprise dawn attack at Tel-el-Kebir.

In 1883 British control was established when Sir Evelyn Baring (Lord Cromer) went to Cairo as Consul-General of Egypt. Arabi, meanwhile, had been sent into exile. Gladstone would not accept that he was genuinely popular. After Tel-el-Kebir and the collapse of popular support for the defeated colonel, he said to the House of Commons:

**8** *The absurdity of supposing that the movement in Egypt was a national one and that Arabi was its soul, has been fully exposed* [shown to be false] *... Arabi is one of the greatest villains alive.*

W. E. Gladstone, speaking to the House of Commons, Hansard, 1882

Other Britons, however, had a quite different opinion of him. For example, Francis Adams wrote:

**9** *Arabi, who was a* fellah *himself and the first one to have risen from the ranks ... came to concentrate the vague hatred and resentment of endless suffering that seethed in the* [Egyptian] *race ...*

Francis Adams, *The New Egypt*, 1893

1 Draw a timeline for the period 1840 to 1890. Use it to show the following events: the death of Muhammad Ali, 1849; the opening of the Suez canal, 1869; the purchase of the Suez Canal shares, 1875; Britain and France take control of Egyptian finances, 1879; Arabi's revolt and the bombardment of Alexandria, 1882; the Battle of Tel-el-Kebir, 1882; Evelyn Baring becomes Consul-General of Egypt, 1883.

2 What was Arabi's revolt about?

3 Put source 8 into your own words to make its meaning clear.

4 Why should Gladstone wish to suggest (source 8) that Arabi did not really have popular support? What evidence is there that he was wrong?

# The Sudan, 1881–98

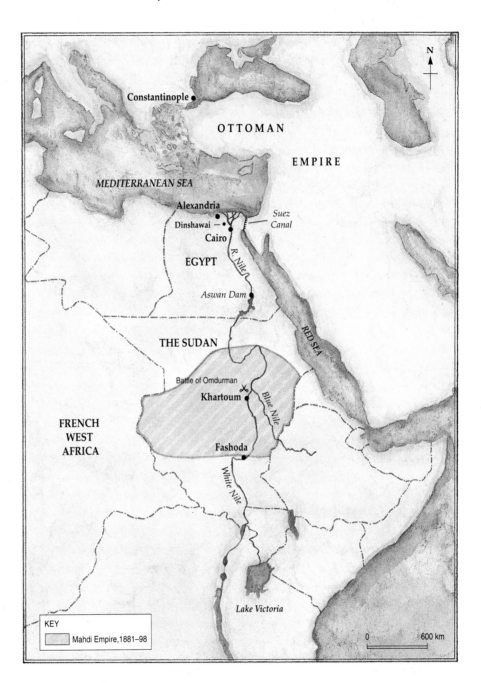

**10** Egypt and the Sudan at the end of the nineteenth century, showing the strategic importance of the upper waters of the Nile, and the threat of foreign intervention.

If Egypt gave Gladstone sleepless nights, the Sudan was a nightmare for him. Without the waters of the Nile, Egypt would be desert. This was why whoever ruled in Egypt had to keep one eye on events in the Sudan, through which the great river flowed on its way to Egypt. Muhammad Ali had tried to bring this huge, sparsely populated country under Egyptian control earlier in the century. But the number of Egyptian officials was small; they had few powers and they were disliked by the Sudanese.

**11** The Mahdi.

## The Mahdi

When the British took control of Egypt in 1882, the most powerful man in the Sudan was Muhammad Ahmed, a Sudanese and a devout Muslim whom his followers called 'Mahdi' ('the One guided by God'). He wanted to reform the whole Muslim world and drive the Egyptians from the Sudan.

His enthusiastic followers, whom the British called 'Dervishes', destroyed an Egyptian army led by British officers in 1883. Gladstone thought it best for Egypt and Britain to pull out of the Sudan completely, and sent

**12** The final moments of General Gordon at Khartoum, as seen by an artist in the *Illustrated London News*.

General Charles Gordon to Khartoum to see how the evacuation of the remaining Egyptian garrisons could best be organised. However, Gordon was besieged by the Mahdi's troops and, finally, killed in Khartoum. A British relief expedition arrived just too late to save him.

Although Gladstone was bitterly criticised at the time – 'Murderer of Gordon', he was called – he stuck by his decision and withdrew all British and Egyptian forces from the Sudan.

Not until 1896 did British and Egyptian forces again march southwards up the Nile. This time they had two enemies. One was the Mahdi's successor. The other was the French, who were pushing eastwards towards the Upper Nile (see source 10). General Kitchener first defeated the Mahdist forces at Omdurman in 1898, and then, the same year, confronted Captain Marchand and a small French force who had raised their country's flag at Fashoda. The French were forced to retire (see also Chapter 5).

**13** **The Battle of Omdurman, 1898.**

32

**14** The British and French discussing the situation at Fashoda.

Britain called the newly conquered country the Anglo-Egyptian Sudan, as if it was jointly ruled. In fact, Britain was much the senior partner. The Governor-General, senior civil servants and army officers were all British.

1 **Link correctly the following dates, people and places:**

| 1883 | Sir Evelyn Baring | Fashoda |
| 1884–5 | General Kitchener | Cairo |
| 1898 | General Gordon | Omdurman |
| 1898 | Captain Marchand | Khartoum |

2 **Why was the Sudan important to Egypt?**

3 **Fashoda was a ruined fort in the middle of nowhere. Why, then, did Britain and France nearly go to war over it?**

4 **Explain the cartoon (source 14). In particular, explain the person up the tree!**

# British Rule in Egypt, 1882–1914

The British had come to Egypt in force to defeat Arabi. In 1914, thirty-two years later, they were still there. There were three main reasons why they stayed. The first was to make sure that the finances of the country were run in such a way that they debts owed by the Khedive's government to the European bond-holders were repaid. The second was to keep the Suez Canal in friendly hands. The third, which was linked to the first two, was to keep the Khedive in power as a puppet ruler, since a nationalist government was likely to be anti-British.

## Sir Evelyn Baring (Lord Cromer)

The real ruler of Egypt from 1882 to 1907, though his title was merely British Agent and Consul-General, was Sir Evelyn Baring, known as Lord Cromer after 1892. A cousin of the Khedive Abbas II told how once, when she was visiting him, they heard sounds in the street outside:

**15** *The Khedive paled. 'Listen', he said, 'I hear the cry of the runner in front of Baring's carriage. Who knows what he is coming to tell me.'*

Quoted by James Morris, *Pax Britannica*, 1968

Abbas II was in no doubt where real power lay. He was heard to say that:

**16** *He realised that he might sit on the box of the state coach but not touch the reins.*

Quoted in the entry on Lord Cromer, *Dictionary of National Biography*, 1921

Cromer was a leading figure in British public life and colonial administration, the son of an MP and a member of a leading banking family. He was serious, balanced and unflappable, with an unshakable confidence in the merits of his decisions.

**17** Abbas II, the Khedive of Egypt (top) and Lord Cromer (Sir Evelyn Baring), the British Agent and Consul-General. Their photographs appeared in the *Illustrated London News* of 28 January 1893.

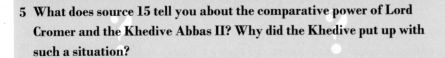

**5** What does source 15 tell you about the comparative power of Lord Cromer and the Khedive Abbas II? Why did the Khedive put up with such a situation?

As far as Britain was concerned, Cromer did a brilliant job. He moved the country's finances out of debt into surplus. The *fellahin* still paid taxes, but they were lower and more fairly collected. He brought to an end a hated system of forced labour. He introduced irrigation schemes and had a great dam built at Aswan. Cotton and sugar production immediately increased, which also improved Egypt's finances.

From the Egyptian point of view, his work looks less impressive. Those who did best out of his financial reforms were the European bondholders and the occupying British forces. From 1882 to 1914, the Egyptian government gained nothing at all from the Suez Canal. While raw cotton production improved, Cromer prevented an Egyptian textile industry from developing in case it damaged the British textile industry. He did little for public services such as education.

## Egyptian nationalism

Cromer did not understand Egyptian nationalism, nor how his actions and those of the British government angered the nationalists. His opinion displayed the attitude of racial superiority typical of his generation:

> **18** [Giving political power to a nationalist would be] *only a little less absurd than the nomination of some savage Red Indian to be Governor-General of Canada.*
>
> Quoted by James Morris, *Pax Britannica*, 1968

Yet most nationalists were educated city-dwellers, lawyers, doctors, teachers and civil servants. They had able leaders like Mustapha Kamil and Saad Zaghlul, and Arabic newspapers to spread their ideas.

The nationalists disliked many things about British rule, especially the way the British often said they would leave soon, but never did. To make matters worse, they made Egyptians pay for the costs of their occupation, and this was another grievance. Then there was the fact that the Suez Canal made no money for Egypt. There was bitterness, too, that when Britain took control of the Sudan in 1898, the army which did the fighting was mainly Egyptian.

## The Dinshawai Incident, 1906

Anti-British feeling rose sharply as a result of events at the village of Dinshawai in 1906. Officers of the British army went pigeon-shooting there. Since pigeons were a source of food for the villagers, the usual custom, which the officers ignored, was to ask permission before starting the shoot. When a barn caught fire during the day's hectic sport, the angry villagers attacked the officers, one of whom was already seriously ill from sunstroke. He died, and the British officials decided to treat his death as murder. They organised a special court,

**19** Saad Zaghlul, the Egyptian nationalist leader.

**20** The Dinshawai Incident.

tried 52 men in the space of half an hour, found four of them guilty, and hanged them in front of the villagers.

There was widespread rioting throughout the country and a folk-song was written which went like this:

**21** *They fell upon Dinshawai*
*And spared neither man nor his brother*
*Slowly they hanged the one and flogged the other.*
*It was a gloomy day when Zaran was killed,*
*His mother from the roof watched, while tears from her were spilled.*
*His brother, O you people, stood by him,*
*And gazed till his eyes grew dim.*

Quoted in Longman, *The Making of Modern Africa*, Vol. 1, 1986

By now, most Egyptians really hated British rule and thought that the sooner it came to an end, the better. They had some years to wait, for although Britain granted Egypt independence in 1922, British troops did not finally leave until the Suez crisis of 1956.

**1 What were the main criticisms of British rule by Egyptian nationalists between 1906 and 1914?**

# 4 Southern Africa

South Africa was unlike both Egypt and India. The growth of the British Empire there was a three-way struggle between the British, the Boers (white people of mainly Dutch descent) and the original black inhabitants. The black, mainly Bantu-speaking peoples of Southern Africa always greatly outnumbered the whites. The first Boers had settled there in the middle of the seventeenth century – long before the British, who came in numbers only after 1820. The meeting of Bantu, Boers and Britons began a violent and tragic story, the results of which are still being worked out today.

## Black people, Boers and British before 1870

The first white settlers arrived in South Africa in 1652. They got the name 'Boer' from the Dutch word for farmer. Their plan was to grow vegetables and other crops, but conditions soon turned them into pastoral farmers. From their settlement, Cape Town, they fanned out northwards and eastwards with their cattle and sheep.

The first indigenous inhabitants they met were the Khoisan, a nomadic people who had been in this part of Africa even longer than the Bantu. Some Khoisan had herds of cattle and flocks of sheep, while others lived by hunting and gathering. Unable to resist either European diseases or the weapons of the settlers, the Khoisan were virtually wiped out. Those who did not die or take refuge in the inland mountains or deserts became servants on white farms.

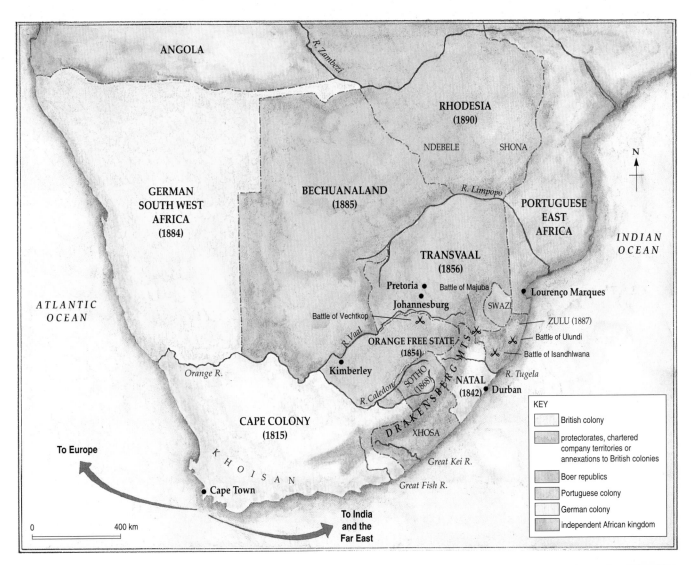

**1** South Africa in 1895, showing the political divisions and the main areas of population settlement.

Map labels:

ANGOLA

R. Zambezi

RHODESIA
(1890)

NDEBELE    SHONA

GERMAN
SOUTH WEST
AFRICA
(1884)

BECHUANALAND
(1885)

R. Limpopo

PORTUGUESE
EAST
AFRICA

INDIAN
OCEAN

TRANSVAAL
(1856)

Pretoria ●    Battle of Majuba    ● Lourenço Marques

Johannesburg    SWAZI

ATLANTIC
OCEAN

Battle of Vechtkop    ZULU (1887)

R. Vaal    ORANGE FREE STATE
(1854)    Battle of Ulundi

Battle of Isandhlwana

Orange R.    Kimberley    R. Tugela

R. Caledon    SOTHO
(1868)    NATAL
(1842)    ● Durban

DRAKENSBERG MTS.

CAPE COLONY
(1815)    XHOSA

K H O I S A N    Great Kei R.

To Europe    Great Fish R.

● Cape Town

0    400 km

To India
and the
Far East

KEY

☐ British colony

☐ protectorates, chartered
company territories or
annexations to British colonies

☐ Boer republics

☐ Portuguese colony

☐ German colony

☐ independent African kingdom

**2** This picture of Boers and Khoisan hunters was painted in about 1820.

**3** Xhosa life and dress in the early nineteenth century.

1 At the time of the first European settlement, who were the indigenous inhabitants of
  a) the south-west region of South Africa?
  b) the more easterly coastlands?
2 What was Britain's main interest in South Africa before 1860?

Once the whites reached the Great Fish River (source 1) they began to meet the Bantu-speaking tribes like the Xhosa (source 3), who were livestock farmers like themselves. As soon as they met, white fought black for the best farming land.

When the British arrived in the early nineteenth century, their chief interest was the harbours along the coast. These were on the main sea route to India before the opening of the Suez Canal. The British took possession of the best port, Cape Town, in 1815 and the other good one, Durban, in 1842. Cape Town became the capital of the Cape Colony. Around Durban there grew up a separate colony, Natal. Some Britons came to settle, especially in the 1820s, but never in numbers to equal the Boers. They soon found themselves in conflict with both the Boers and the indigenous peoples.

## Boer attitudes towards black people

To the British, the way the Boers treated their black and coloured servants seemed virtual slavery – a system abolished throughout the Empire in 1833. Although the British government did not support equality between black and white, it wanted greater freedom and better treatment for South Africa's black peoples.

Rather than accept British reforms, tens of thousands of Boers left the Cape Colony and created two new Boer republics, the Orange Free State and the South African Republic (Transvaal). Their tough, well-armed mounted commandos and their well-defended 'laagers' – camps defended by wagons drawn up in a circle – were too strong for the black tribes. The Boers got the farmland they wanted. Firmly believing that God had created black people inferior to them, they used them as servants and labourers. The Transvaal constitution of 1858 forbade:

**4** *equality between coloured people and white inhabitants either in church or state.*

Bernard Porter, *The Lion's Share*, 1984

Like the Boers, the British fought the black peoples for their land. In a long series of wars between 1815 and 1870, they gradually took possession of the coastal lands between Cape Town and Durban.

**3** Explain the main reasons for conflict between:
Boers and black people;
Boers and British;
British and black people.

**4** After studying source 5, explain why the Boers, though usually outnumbered, won more battles than they lost against black people in the nineteenth century.

**5** The Battle of Vechtkop, 1836.

# Diamonds and gold

The British became much more interested in South Africa with the discovery of diamonds and gold. The richest diamond fields in the world, near Kimberley on the edge of the Cape Colony, were opened up in 1866. Then, in 1886, came the discovery of the richest goldfields in the world on the Rand in the middle of the Transvaal. If these riches were to be developed, both black people and Boers must come more firmly under British rule.

**6** The first of the gold mines on the Rand near Johannesburg. Eventually these would run as deep as five miles below the surface. Note that most of the heavy mining work was done by blacks.

In 1874, Disraeli's government came up with the idea of uniting the white (British and Boer) colonies in a single federation or union. Lord Carnarvon, the Colonial Secretary, suggested that the main reason for uniting was the 'problem' of the black people:

**7** *The most immediately urgent reason for general union is the formidable character* [great difficulty] *of the native question, and the importance of a uniform, wise and strong policy in dealing with it.*

Quoted by C. W. de Kiewiet, *A History of South Africa*, 1941

**1** What happened in 1866 and 1886 to make Britain much more interested in South Africa?

**2** What was Carnarvon's federation plan (see source 7)? Who had to be defeated for it to have any chance of success?

**3  How did the British deal with the Zulu problem? Did it help bring the Boers into a federation with Britain?**

# The Zulu War, 1878–9

In the early 1820s the Zulu kingdom, on the coast north-east of Natal, had been turned into a formidable war machine by King Shaka. Young warriors were taught that they did not properly become men until they had 'washed their spears' in the blood of an enemy. Highly disciplined, astonishingly brave and drilled to fight at close quarters with short stabbing spears called assegais, they terrified their enemies and had seldom tasted defeat. They won a victory over the British at Isandhlwana in 1879, when one column of Lord Chelmsford's invading army was surprised and virtually annihilated. After this defeat, however, the British destroyed the Zulu army at Ulundi and, in due course, added Zululand to the Empire.

The main British aim in defeating the Zulus was to persuade the Boer republics that it would be in their interest to join the strong British Empire. In fact, the conquest of Zululand had the opposite effect. In 1877, Britain had taken over the bankrupt South African Republic. Now that the Zulus were no longer a danger, the Boers rebelled against British rule and defeated a British force at Majuba in 1881. The newly elected government of Gladstone decided to make peace and agree to Boer independence.

**8  Retreat from Isandhlwana: this picture appeared in a British magazine in 1879.**

# Cecil Rhodes, the millionaire imperialist

The first miners at Kimberly had worked numerous small claims (source 9), but later the shrewder businessmen formed larger companies which bought out the smaller operators. Eventually, in 1888, the De Beers Company won monopoly (total) control of the diamond industry.

In 1889 Cecil Rhodes, head of De Beers and a central figure in South Africa's economic and political life, formed the British South Africa Company to open up new mines in the area between the Limpopo and Zambezi rivers (see source 1). The fact that these lands were occupied by the Ndebele and Shona peoples did not matter to him, especially when he heard that the Transvaal Boers were interested in the same area.

Men from Rhodes's company persuaded the Chief of the Ndebele, Lobengula, to sign over to them all the mining rights to his lands. Then the British South Africa Company sent a force of 700 men armed with machine-guns to seize these lands and the lands of the neighbouring Shona. In 1890 they raised the Union Jack at a place which they named Fort Salisbury in honour of Lord Salisbury, the British Prime Minister.

In 1899 the first train to come up the recently completed railway line from Cape Town puffed into Salisbury. The locomotive was called the Cecil J. Rhodes and carried on it the slogan 'Rhodes, Railways and Imperial Expansion'. The new colony, with Salisbury as its capital, was named Rhodesia after its founder, whose money and ambition had formed it.

**9** **The diamond diggings at Kimberley's 'Big Hole' in 1875, showing the network of steel ropes that carried the soil to the surface for sifting.**

Who was this extraordinary man Rhodes? He was an astonishing mixture of businessman, politician and dreamer. He used his diamond wealth to set up a company to develop the Rand goldfields, which made him richer still. From 1890 to 1895 he was Prime Minister of the Cape Colony. What he dreamed about most was a British Empire which stretched without a break from Cape Town to Cairo in Egypt.

As he wrote to a friend:

**10** *I contend that we are the finest race in the world and that the more of the world we inhabit, the better it is for the human race . . . The furtherance [extension] of the British Empire, for the bringing of the whole uncivilised world under British rule, for the recovery of the United States . . . What a dream! But yet it is probable . . .*

Cecil J. Rhodes, Letter to W. T. Stead, 19 August 1891

The British government, though it did not share Rhodes's fantastic ambitions, usually supported him. It had two main reasons: first, the scramble for Africa had begun (see page 11) and, wherever they raised the Union Jack, Rhodes and his friends prevented rival European countries from gaining a foothold. Second, it wanted the Rand goldfields.

THE RHODES COLOSSUS
STRIDING FROM CAPE TOWN TO CAIRO.

1 Where did Rhodes's money come from?
2 What was his main aim?
3 Explain the cartoon of Rhodes the Colossus (source 11).
4 List five adjectives which can accurately be used about Rhodes.
5 How much had he achieved for the British Empire by 1895?

**11** 'Rhodes the Colossus', a cartoon published in the 1890s. The Colossus of Rhodes was a huge bronze statue, supposed to have stood astride the entrance to the harbour of the island of Rhodes in ancient times. The cartoon refers to Cecil Rhodes's ambition to build a Cape to Cairo railway.

1 What reasons were there to suggest (source 12) that the Transvaal was 'the richest place on earth'?
2 Who ruled the Transvaal in 1899?
3 Who were the *uitlanders*? Explain how
   a) Rhodes and Jameson failed, but
   b) Milner succeeded in using them against the Transvaal government.

# The causes of the South African War, 1899–1902

In the 1890s, the South African Republic (the Transvaal), previously a poor farming country, was becoming much richer and stronger thanks to the Rand goldfields. As an official in the Colonial Office said:

12 [The Transvaal is already] *the richest place on earth and will soon be the natural capital state of South African commercial, social and political life.*

Quoted by R. E. Robinson and J. A. Gallagher, *Africa and the Victorians*, 1961

Paul Kruger, President of the SAR, distrusted the British in general and Rhodes in particular. He used the money from the goldfields to modernise his army and to build a railway to the sea in the Portuguese colony of Mozambique. He could then do business with the world without having to use the British ports of Durban and Cape Town.

However, the mining experts and businessmen who came to Johannesburg and the goldfields were mainly British and felt badly treated by their Boer rulers. In 1895, Rhodes and his friend Jameson put together an incompetent plot to seize the goldfields. The British in Johannesburg, known as *uitlanders*, or foreigners, were supposed to rise in revolt. As they did so, Jameson would be riding across the Transvaal border to their aid. The *uitlanders* failed to rise and Jameson simply rode into the arms of the Boer army!

The Jameson Raid was a disaster for Rhodes and a setback for Britain. However, with an enthusiastic imperialist as Colonial Secretary, Britain was

13 Lord Alfred Milner and his staff outside Government House, Cape Town.

**4 What were the main reasons for the start of the South African War in 1899?**

not put off for long. Chamberlain named Sir Alfred Milner as High Commissioner in the Cape Colony. In his own much cooler way, Milner was as keen an imperialist as Chamberlain. He looked for a way to provoke the Boers into war.

Milner stirred up the *uitlanders* on the Rand against Kruger, and then stirred up public opinion in Britain in support of the *uitlanders*. He demanded that Britain should come to their aid. Finally, Milner made sure that his long negotiations with Kruger in search of a peaceful compromise failed. The Boers decided that war was bound to come and their best chance was to strike first, hoping to gain victory before Britain could call in reinforcements from other parts of the Empire. In October 1899, they declared war.

## The course of the war

**14** The South African War, showing the Boer and British campaigns, and the main battles.

Two tiny republics of farmers declaring war on the greatest empire in the world: it seemed absurd. The editor of the *Daily Telegraph* was 'in doubt whether to laugh or to weep'.

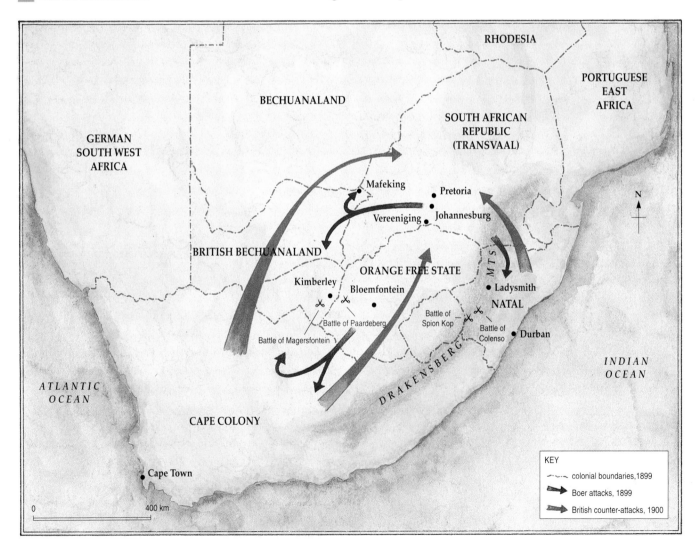

**15** The battle of Paardeberg, painted by Sylvester Reisacher.

**16** This French cartoon, published in 1902, showed the English general, Kitchener, as an enormous toad.

The war lasted longer than anyone expected, however, and both sides suffered huge losses. At first the Boers won some spectacular victories, notably at Spion Kop (source 14), but no European nation came to their aid (Kruger had hoped that Germany would take his side) and soon British reinforcements poured in from all over the Empire.

Early in 1900 General Roberts forced the surrender of a Boer army at Paardeberg and swept northwards. In May, the news of the relief of Mafeking, where the British had been besieged for six months, was received with hysterical joy in London. In June, Roberts raised the Union Jack in Pretoria.

To Britain's surprise, the war was not over. The Boers continued fighting, using the guerrilla tactics of raids and ambushes. General Kitchener decided to counter these tactics by pinning the mobile Boer horsemen down with barbed wire and concrete forts. He also herded Boer women and children into concentration camps.

Those in charge of the camps failed to set even the most basic standards of hygiene and, before a public outcry led by Emily Hobhouse and some Liberal politicians took effect, 28,000 Boer women and children died there from disease. Finally, in May 1902, the Boers gave up and made peace by the

Treaty of Vereeniging. At the cost of 20,000 British, 35,000 Boer and 14,000 African lives – and £200 million – Britain had won the South African War. The Transvaal and Orange Free State became part of the British Empire, and so did the Rand gold mines.

1 **Put the following topics into correct chronological order and write brief notes on each:**
   **the concentration camps**
   **the Boers begin guerrilla war**
   **the relief of Mafeking**
   **the Treaty of Vereeniging**
   **Roberts raises the Union Jack at Pretoria**
   **the Battle of Paardeberg.**

2 **Why does the French cartoon in source 16 show Kitchener, one of Britain's best generals, as an enormous toad?**

3 **European newspapers were very anti-British during the South African War. Why do you think this was so?**

# The situation of black people

Blacks provided the cheap labour which made possible the rapid growth of both diamond and gold mining. White governments used taxes and labour laws to force black people to work on the mines. Generally speaking, South African governments gave the mine owners what they wanted. The policy of the Johannesburg Chamber of Mines was as follows:

17 *Work among whites must be confined* [kept] *to skilled departments . . . the expansion of the mines and prosperity, contentment and existence of the white population depend . . . on an adequate supply of cheap labour through the coloured races.*

Report of the Johannesburg Chamber of Mines, 1902

So began the pattern of black migrant labour and white-owned industry which became such a typical part of South African life in the twentieth century.

## Black political rights

In the Cape Colony, black men could vote in elections if they owned some property and had some education. The number voting was small compared to the whites, but was growing. So, too, was black political awareness. The first black political association started in the Cape Colony in 1880, the first black newspaper in 1884.

During the South African War, most blacks supported Britain. They knew that the Boers fiercely opposed any political rights for blacks, and they thought that the British would give them a better deal.

The opposite happened. Feeling guilty about the effects of the war on the Boers, and believing that British rule could not survive in the long run without Boer support, British governments aimed to win the support of the defeated Boers. In 1910 Britain granted self-governmnet to the Union of South Africa. Since there were more Boers than British, and only the small number of black people in the Cape had the right to vote, the new Union had a Boer majority which continued to believe that blacks should only be servants and workers.

Nine of the black political leaders went to London in 1909 to try – without success – to persuade Britain to protect their rights. They failed because the British Parliament thought it more important to gain the friendship of the Boers.

Educated blacks realised that only through unity and organisation would they gain political rights in their own country. In 1912, they founded the South African Native National Congress. J. I. Dube, a headteacher who had completed his education in the USA, became President, S. T. Plaatje, a journalist, its Secretary and P. K. I. Seme, a lawyer, its Treasurer.

**18** The SANNC delegation in London.

**19** The Land Act, 1913: this shows the amount of land available for black ownership.

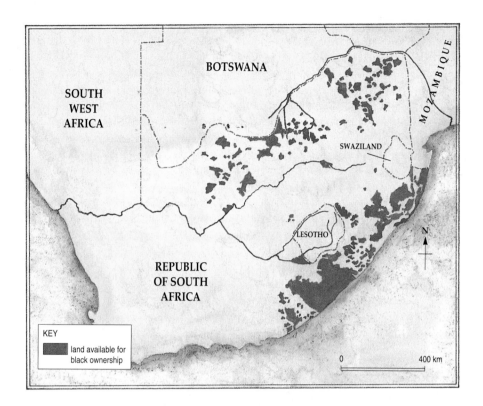

In 1913, the new Union government passed a Land Act which ended the right of blacks to own land in white areas. The Act limited black-owned land to the so-called reserves, which amounted to about 7 per cent of South Africa (see source 19). Many black farmers could no longer farm the land they had lived on for years. Instead, they were driven off to seek mining or other work in the towns, or to scratch a living in the overcrowded reserves. The SANNC sent another delegation to London to try to persuade Parliament to stop the Land Act being passed. This delegation also failed and the blacks felt badly betrayed by Britain.

# Review and Assessment

**1** Lord Milner, who had worked for Cromer in Egypt wrote in 1892:

> **1** *It would be difficult to over-estimate what the work of England in Egypt owes to Cromer . . . Slowly but surely he gained his main points. He has realised that the essence of our policy in Egypt is to help the Egyptians to work out their own salvation.*

Al-Ahram, an Egyptian nationalist newspaper, in 1907 when Cromer left Egypt:

> **2** *He has been a violent destroyer and tyrant. He destroyed the Egyptian Sudan and built an English Sudan. He destroyed the Egyptian government and built up an English advisory body.*

Re-read pages 29–30 and study sources 1–3 on this page.

**a** What did Cromer do for the Egyptians in Egypt rather than for the English in Egypt?

**b** What kind of bias would you look for in the comments of Milner and Al-Ahram (sources 1 and 2) about Cromer? What evidence, if any, can you find to support each source.

**3** The Aswan Dam, Egypt.

**2** Cecil Rhodes, speaking in the Cape Town parliament in 1894 about the blacks of South Africa.

> **4** *If you are one who really loves the natives, you must make them worthy of the country they live in . . . You will certainly not make them worthy if you allow them to sit in idleness and if you do not train them in the arts of civilization.*

Re-read pages 42–8.

**a** What evidence can you find of the 'idleness' of South Africa's blacks? What did Rhodes mean by the 'arts of civilization'?

**b** What, above all, did the black nationalist leaders want from the South African and British parliaments between 1902 and 1914?

# 5 Expansion after 1870

There were many reasons for the growth of the British and other European empires at the end of the nineteenth century. The most important reasons were economic or strategic. European nations created empires in the hope of getting richer. They also took possession of land overseas to protect what they had already, or to prevent their European rivals gaining more.

The three case studies in the previous chapters – India, Egypt and South Africa – show both economic and strategic motives at work. India mattered to Britain mainly for economic reasons centred on trade. Egypt mattered for strategic reasons, because it guarded the main sea-route to India through the Suez Canal. South Africa mattered for both strategic and economic reasons: at first for its harbours on the old sea-route to India, and later for its wealth in diamonds and gold.

## Economic reasons

The advertisement on page 52 appeared in the British press in 1887. Pears' soap was the most heavily advertised soap in Britain in the later years of the nineteenth century. In their joky way, Pears' advertisers show trade and the expansion of the Empire going hand in hand.

Clearly, trade was a major reason for the growth of the British Empire. In this example, the ever-increasing demand for soap in Britain led to trade in palm oil, from which the soap was made. British interest in the lower reaches of the Niger River, where the oil was produced, led George Goldie to set up the

## Good Complexion! AND Nice Hands!

NOTHING adds so much to personal attractions as a bright, clear complexion, and a soft skin. Without them the handsomest and most regular features are but coldly impressive, whilst with them the plainest become attractive; and yet there is no advantage so easily secured. The regular use of a properly prepared Soap is one of the chief means; but the Public have not the requisite knowledge of the manufacture of Soap to guide them to a proper selection, so a pretty box, a pretty colour, or an agreeable perfume too frequently outweighs the more important consideration, viz.: *the Composition of the Soap itself*, and thus many a good complexion is spoiled which would be enhanced by proper care.

*A most Eminent Authority on the Skin,*
### Professor Sir Erasmus Wilson, F.R.S.,
Writes in the JOURNAL OF CUTANEOUS MEDICINE :—

"THE use of a good Soap is certainly calculated to preserve the Skin in "health, to maintain its complexion and tone, and prevent its falling "into wrinkles. PEARS is a name engraved on the memory of the "oldest inhabitant; and PEARS' Transparent SOAP is an article of the "nicest and most careful manufacture, and one of the most refreshing "and agreeable of balms for the Skin."

TO persons whose skin is delicate or sensitive to changes in the weather, winter or summer, PEARS' TRANSPARENT SOAP is invaluable, as, on account of its emollient, non-irritant character, *Redness, Roughness and Chopping are prevented*, and a clear appearance and soft velvety condition maintained, and a good, healthful and attractive complexion ensured. Its agreeable and lasting perfume, beautiful appearance, and soothing properties, commend it as the greatest luxury and most elegant adjunct to the toilet.

*Testimonial from*
### Madame Adelina Patti.
"I HAVE found PEARS' SOAP matchless for the Hands and Complexion."

*Adelina Patti*

**PEARS'** Transparent SOAP.

**TABLETS & BALLS:** 1s. each. Larger Sizes, 1s. 6d. and 2s. 6d. *(The 2s. 6d. Tablet is perfumed with Otto of Roses.)* A smaller Tablet (unscented) is sold at 6d.

**PEARS'** Transparent SOAP.

THE FORMULA OF BRITISH CONQUEST

PEARS' SOAP IS THE BEST

REGᵈ COPYRIGHT

**PEARS' SOAP IN THE SOUDAN.**
"Even if our invasion of the Soudan has done nothing else it has at any rate left the Arab something to puzzle his fuzzy head over, for the legend **PEARS' SOAP IS THE BEST,** *inscribed in huge white characters on the rock which marks the farthest point of our advance towards Berber,* will tax all the wits of the Dervishes of the Desert to translate."—Phil Robinson, *War Correspondent (in the Soudan) of the Daily Telegraph in London,* 1884.

**1** **An advertisement for Pears' soap, 1887.**

Royal Niger Company in 1886. The company soon gained a monopoly of the palm-oil trade.

Every region of the Empire offers an example of the importance of trade. The East India Company started buying precious stones and hand-made luxury cloth in India to sell in Britain and Europe; it stayed to open up a huge market in India for British goods, especially factory-made cotton clothes. Hong Kong and Singapore flourished on the China trade, Malaya produced rubber and South Africa gold. Egyptian cotton was shipped to Britain to be woven into clothes and then exported all over the world. In 1909, the Liberal MP for Bolton, a cotton manufacturing town in Lancashire, had no doubt why

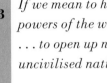

1 Where and when did the Pears' soap advertisement appear? Does the advertisement aim to sell soap to the British or to the Sudanese? What do the advertisers think about the Empire?

2 In source 2, what is the Liberal MP supporting? What did Egypt produce which was particularly useful to Lancashire businessmen?

3 Put source 3 into your own words to make its meaning clear. What, in Lord Salisbury's opinion, is the main reason for empire-building?

he was an imperialist. Britain had to stay in Egypt, he told the House of Commons:

> **2** *You may say that we in Lancashire are selfish. But we have to look after our business.*
>
> Hansard, Fifth Series, 19 (1909)

British policy in Southern Africa was shaped increasingly by economic motives (see also pages 40–5). Politicians as well as businessmen believed that the Empire was vital to the nation's economic health. Lord Salisbury, the Conservative Prime Minister, wrote in 1895:

> **3** *If we mean to hold our own against the efforts of all the civilised powers of the world to strangle our commerce . . . we must be prepared . . . to open up new markets for ourselves among the half-civilised or uncivilised nations of the globe.*
>
> Quoted by B. H. Brown, *The Tariff Reform Movement in Great Britain*

# Strategic reasons

Strategic aims had much to do with the expansion of the British Empire after 1870. This was because British trade had expanded across the globe in the first half of the nineteenth century without a serious threat from any direction. After 1870, however, European rivals like France, Germany and Russia wanted more trade and land for themselves and threatened Britain's existing empire. Consequently, British governments hurried to take control of many parts of Africa and Asia rather than let them fall under the influence of rival nations. Businessmen supported this policy. For example, in 1884 Glasgow merchants complained to Lord Granville, the Foreign Secretary, about the Germans in the Cameroons:

> **4** *The Directors of the Chamber of Commerce view with alarm the annexation* [taking] *by Germany of this district, which for many years has been under British protection. Should it be found necessary . . . to allow Germany to take possession of the southern bank of the Cameroons River, it is all important that the northern bank should continue under the protection of, or be formally annexed by, Britain.*
>
> Letter from John McLaren, President of the Chamber of Commerce, to Lord Granville, 10 November 1884

1 Using the maps (sources 5–8), decide which European countries seemed to be threatening Britain's position
   a) in India,
   b) in Egypt and the Suez Canal,
   c) in the Upper Nile,
   d) in South Africa?
2 What new colonies did Britain acquire in each of these areas between 1870 and 1914?

The strategic problems varied from one part of the Empire to another, but they usually led to it getting bigger. These maps show what happened in four key areas:

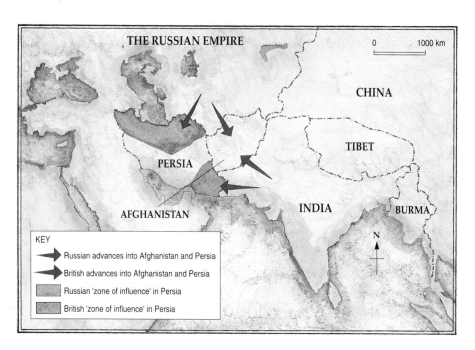

**5** India: fear of Russia leads to British forces entering Persia, Afghanistan and Tibet.

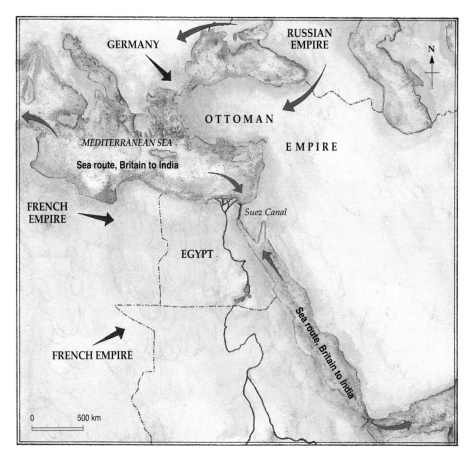

**6** Egypt: after 1882, the expanding empires of Germany, Russia and France began to be a threat to Britain's key route to India through the Suez Canal.

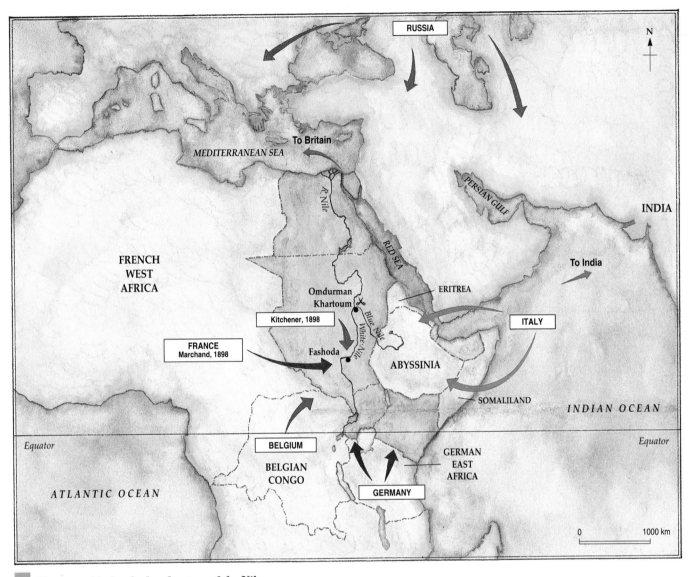

**7**  **The scramble for the headwaters of the Nile.**

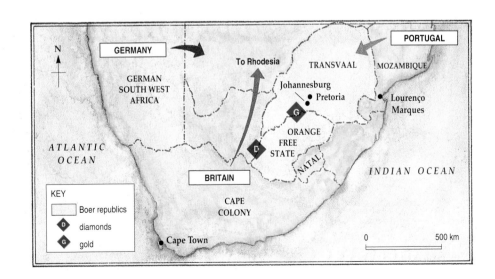

**8**  **The European nations and Southern Africa.**

1 Explain the cartoon (source 10). What happened to the frog in 1898?

## The Fashoda crisis, 1898

Events at Fashoda in the valley of the Upper Nile provide a good example of how the new imperial ambitions of other European countries led Britain to acquire more territory for strategic reasons. In this case, French actions caused a strong British reaction, nearly led to war, and in the end added the Sudan (a country covering nearly a million square miles) to the Empire.

Fashoda was a half-ruined fort in a desolate spot a long way up the Nile from Egypt. It stood at a place where, so a French scientist suggested, a dam could be built which would control the flow of the Nile downstream to Egypt. The French, very angry after the British takeover of Egypt, wished to show that they, too, could add to their colonies. They already had a large empire in North and West Africa and tried to enlarge it eastwards (source 7). In 1897 they ordered Captain Marchand, with 12 French and 150 Senegalese troops, to march east from West Africa and claim the Upper Nile for France.

The British government saw this as a direct threat to their position in Egypt. They ordered Kitchener, who had already marched to Khartoum and defeated the Mahdi's followers at Omdurman, to proceed up-river to Fashoda. He arrived with 5 gunboats, 100 British and 2,500 Sudanese troops. Eventually, after much argument and bad feeling between France and Britain, Marchand had to retreat. The French realised that, as their Foreign Minister Delcassé put it:

9 *We've only got arguments, they've got the troops.*

Quoted by James Morris, *Farewell the Trumpets*, 1978

10 'A frog he would a-roving go, whether Britannia would let him or no: Niger to Fashoda Moonshine, 5 March 1898.'

# Population growth

Economic and strategic motives were not the only reasons for the expansion of the Empire. The growth of Britain's population also played its part.

**11** An emigrant ship leaving Britain. This engraving appeared in *The Graphic*, 18 December 1869.

Millions of Britons emigrated from Britain, helping the Empire to grow and to develop. Cecil Rhodes was sure that, without an Empire, Britain faced disaster. He wrote:

**12** *In order to save the 40 million inhabitants of the United Kingdom from a bloody civil war, we colonial statesmen must acquire [get] new lands to settle the surplus population . . .*

Quoted by B. Semmel, *Imperialism and Social Reform*, 1960

1 Why did people like Livingstone give their lives to difficult and often dangerous mission work?

2 How might historians set about finding out how important these humanitarian 'do-gooding' ideas were in the expansion of the British Empire?

Despite Rhodes's emphasis on 'new lands', most emigrants who left Britain to settle permanently overseas went to countries where the climate was not too extreme nor the indigenous people too frightening. The popular destinations were the USA, Canada, Australia and New Zealand. Few emigrants went to India, Egypt and tropical Africa. Britons went to those parts of the world to trade, to take raw materials like rubber or precious stones, or to rule. They did not put down permanent roots. 'Home' remained Britain, where they sent their children to be educated and where they themselves retired. The only African colonies which attracted settlers in any numbers were Kenya, Rhodesia and South Africa.

# Humanitarian reasons

Many Britons wanted to convert other nations to Christianity and 'civilise' them. They helped to make the Empire grow because they believed that would make the world a better place. David Livingstone, for example, was world famous as a missionary and explorer by the time he died on the shores of Lake Tanganyika in 1873. He had given his life to the task of bringing to Africa the three Cs: Christianity, Commerce and Civilisation. The more he travelled in Central Africa, the more determined he became to get rid of the slave trade which still flourished there.

13 'The meeting of Livingstone and Stanley in Central Africa'. This drawing appeared in *The Graphic*, 30 April 1890. The artist used sketches and information supplied by Stanley.

**14** Missionary work in the Empire.

Christian missionaries sometimes upset non-Christian peoples more than British governments wished. In the late nineteenth century, therefore, keen imperialists tended to stress Civilisation rather than Christianity. Rudyard Kipling, born in India and the most popular poet in Britain in the 1890s, put into verse the idea of 'the White Man's Burden'.

> **15** *Take up the White Man's burden –*
> *Send forth the best ye breed –*
> *Go, bind your sons to exile,*
> *To serve your captive's need;*
> *To wait in heavy harness,*
> *On fluttered folk and wild*
> *Your new-caught, sullen peoples,*
> *Half-devil and half-child.*
>
> Rudyard Kipling, 'The White Man's Burden', 1898

The belief was that the peoples of the Empire, 'half-devil and half-child', with kind but firm guidance from the best type of Briton, would become less bad and more grown-up!

# Technological reasons

Finally, a technological reason helps to explain why the British Empire, and the empires of other European nations, grew so fast between 1870 and 1914. A technological gap had opened up between the advanced industrial nations and the rest of the world. The poet Hilaire Belloc summed it up neatly like this:

> **16** *Whatever happens we have got*
> *The Maxim gun and they have not.*
>
> Quoted by James Morris, *Pax Britannica*, 1975

The Maxim gun was an early but effective machine gun which made possible the defeat of Lobengula's warlike Ndebele by a few hundred soldiers of the British South Africa Company. Ironclad gunboats helped to smash the massed attacks of the Mahdi's followers at Omdurman. In battle after battle, skirmish after skirmish, small but well-armed British forces destroyed thousands of the enemy, usually with few losses. Defeats only happened when generals were careless and their troops were ambushed or caught by surprise. Moreover, steamships and railways made it possible to bring in reinforcements quickly when trouble broke out.

1 Look at source 13 on page 31. What are the main technological advantages of the British forces?

2 What was a Maxim gun? Why was it so useful in imperial wars?

3 In what important ways was the technology of Britain advanced compared to that of Africa and Asia?

# 6 Aspects of Imperial Rule

## How the Empire was run

**1** Queen Victoria giving a Bible to an African Chief.

Victoria, the Queen-Empress, was the Empire's sovereign or head. Parliament in London made its laws and decided its main policies. Although by 1870 it had allowed white settler countries like Canada and Australia to have their own parliaments and to make many of their own decisions, it ruled its Asian and African colonies much more directly and strictly. This reflected the ideas of racial superiority which were part of the creed of imperialism, as we shall see.

**2** The administrative heart of the Empire, Whitehall.

Inside their headquarters in London's Whitehall (source 2) worked the men who ran the colonies. The India Office took care of India, the less grand Colonial Office looked after everywhere else. An important task of the civil servants in Whitehall was to choose the men who would rule the colonies on a practical, day-to-day basis.

These colonial officers were almost all from the same social background: they had been educated at public schools and at the universities of Oxford or Cambridge. They shared the same values. They saw themselves as confident, courageous and honest. They believed in hard work, justice and service. They also believed Britain to be the most advanced nation in the world, and saw themselves as natural leaders and first-class administrators. It was the opinion of Sir John Strachey, whose family had produced many Indian civil servants, that:

**3** *No country has ever possessed a more admirable body of public servants than the Civil Service of India.*

Quoted by James Morris, *Pax Britannica*, 1975

They needed to be confident, because their responsibilities were enormous. Most started off as district or provincial officers. In India there were hardly more than a thousand of them for a country with 200 million inhabitants. Their main tasks were to keep law and order and to collect taxes, but many other challenges and opportunities came their way too.

Their strengths – in their own eyes, anyway – were their fairness as local magistrates, their readiness to work hard and their determination to do their best for people in their district. Their main weakness was their amazing sense of superiority, which gave them a low opinion of most things Asian and African, and stopped them from treating indigenous people as partners in their work.

1 What does source 1 show?
2 Some people think that the painter did not wish to record an actual meeting, but rather to symbolise (show in pictorial form) important things about the Empire. What do you think he is trying to symbolise?
3 How reliable is source 3 as evidence of the abilities of the Indian Civil Service? Explain your answer. What other evidence could historians use?

**4** A police officer and his men in the Punjab, 1869.

To help him keep the peace, a district commissioner could call in the police. As source 4 shows, the commanding officer of the police might well be British, the rest of his force local inhabitants. Military forces were seldom far away, either. The police and the army were paid for by local taxes and customs duties.

Another method the British used to keep control of their far-flung Empire was to let local rulers whom they could trust stay in charge as long as they kept the peace, paid their taxes and otherwise did what the imperial government wanted. After the Indian Mutiny and Rebellion of 1857–8, British governments made a fuss of the Indian princes and princesses, showering them with honours.

In the large West African colony of Nigeria, the British ruled the mainly Muslim north through the local chiefs. The first British commissioners, George Goldie and Frederick Lugard, believed firmly in leaving the former rulers to follow their old methods of government, as long as they kept the peace and agreed to pay taxes to Britain.

**5** The Maharajah of Jaipur.

# Christianity in the Empire

European Christianity was very energetic in the early nineteenth century. Thousands of white missionaries came to Africa and Asia with the aim of converting the 'heathen'. They were often successful. By 1900, there were more than 12,000 missionaries throughout the Empire who claimed a total of at least 10 million conversions. Some of the boldest missionaries were women, like Ann Taylor in Northern India and Mary Slessor in West Africa.

**6** Women missionaries.

Most missions included schools which played a leading part in educating the local population. In 1876, for example, there were nearly 400 pupils attending the school at the Lovedale mission among the Xhosa people in South Africa. Most missionaries in Africa linked Christianity with commerce and civilisation (by which they meant white customs). The Rev. John Freeman wrote in 1851:

**7** *It is something to have changed the old kraal* [African settlement] *into a decent village . . . idleness into industry, ignorance into intelligence . . . heathenism into Christianity.*

Rev. J. Freeman, *Tour of South Africa*, 1851

With some reason, Africans came to see missionaries as the first sign of a white attack on their lands. When Mwanga, the young Kabaka of Buganda (now part of Uganda) heard that the missionary Bishop Hannington was coming to visit him, he and his advisers were alarmed. They told Mackay, another missionary, that:

**8** *white men were all the same and that we and the bishop were only the forerunners of war.*

Thomas Pakenham, *The Scramble for Africa*, 1991

Mwanga had Bishop Hannington killed, but to no avail. He had to sign away his kingdom to Frederick Lugard and his Maxim guns in 1890.

Because white people and their values dominated the Churches, Africans often developed their own forms of Christianity. In the Bible, Africa is called Ethiopia – so, in South Africa and Nigeria, people set up 'Ethiopian' churches. Sometimes they were centres of political protest as well as religious events.

**1** What other religions did Christian missionaries meet in India (see pages 15–17) and Egypt (see page 26)?

**2** When and where did criticism by Christians of other religious customs lead to a serious anti-British revolt (see page18–19)?

**3** Apart from 'converting the heathen' what else pleased the Rev. Freeman (source 7) about the work of the missions in South Africa?

**4** Why did Mwanga of Buganda distrust missionaries like Bishop Hannington (see source 8)? Did he have any good reason for this attitude?

# Racial attitudes

Most Britons in the late nineteenth century never doubted that they were members of a very superior race, nor that Asians and Africans were inferior. Of the Chinese, Captain Osborn of the Royal Navy had this typical opinion:

9 *They are only Asiatics . . . treat them as children; make them do what we know is for their benefit, as well as our own, and all our difficulties in China are at an end.*

V. G. Kiernan, *The Lords of Human Kind*, 1969

10 'Daylight at last'. Note how the British artist shows Stanley as stern, calm and confident, despite having battled through the steaming jungle of Central Africa, and the Africans as excited children.

**3** Why did most Britons in the late nineteenth century think of themselves as members of a superior race?

**4** Looking at source 12, what do you think was the Chinese artist's opinion of the British in the China ports?

Since, in the eyes of most whites, the black and brown peoples were what the imperialist poet Rudyard Kipling called 'lesser breeds without the law', they could not be trusted to rule themselves.

These attitudes existed for a number of reasons. The first was ignorance. Most Britons did not know about the achievements of Asian and African civilisations. They kept themselves separate from the peoples over whom they ruled and knew little of their history or their customs. Their Christianity made them hostile to other religious beliefs. Their undoubted technological superiority led them to believe that they were superior in everything else, too. By applying Charles Darwin's theory of evolution to human societies, they convinced themselves that Western societies had evolved faster than others and were the most advanced. Not surprisingly, when the ruins of a city built by an early African civilisation were discovered at Great Zimbabwe in 1905, Britons refused to believe that it could have been built by Africans. Phoenicians or Arabs, maybe – but not Africans!

These attitudes did Britain no good in the long run, since they angered people who might otherwise have been ready to work in partnership with Britain. An educated Indian explained his feelings in 1866:

**11** *A man that has received a thorough English education is fit for everything which is good and laudable* [praiseworthy] *... [but the British] look upon us as being of an inferior kind ... this conduct tends to demoralise us and estrange us* [make us feel unworthy and like strangers].

Quoted by V. G. Kiernan, *The Lords of Human Kind*, 1969

**12** This Chinese picture of an English sailor was published in 1857.

# Sport

British public schools took sport very seriously and many of the major games of the world were first organised in nineteenth-century Britain. British soldiers, sailors and imperial civil servants took their games around the world with them.

Cricket was *the* imperial game. It took root in the West Indies and India as well as in the white settler lands. The best qualification for working in the Rhodesian civil service was said to be a good batting average. The first Indian club, the Oriental Cricket Club, was formed for members of the Parsee religious group and, by 1912, an annual tournament was contested by four sides: Parsee, Hindu, Muslim and English. By then, England and Australia were playing regular test matches and the West Indies, South Africa and New Zealand all had their inter-district competitions.

The other main sports which Britain exported were horse-racing and

**13** **Cricket in India, 1863.**

The Scoring Table

Coming out

Going in

General view of the match

A Parsee Cricketer

**14** A pig-sticking.

hunting. Calcutta had one of the largest race-courses in the world and the day of the Viceroy's Cup was the high point of the Raj's social season. And the British hunted everything that moved: foxes, pigs, deer, zebra – and, of course, Indian tigers. Many Indians, especially the princes, joined them.

Not all sports started in Britain and spread across the Empire. Polo was played in the Mughal Empire. The British learnt it in India and founded the Calcutta Polo Club in the 1860s.

# Supporters of the Empire

The Empire was at its most popular in the 1880s and 1890s, during the years of the Scramble for Africa. Of all Britain's Colonial Secretaries, Joseph Chamberlain (1890–5) was the keenest imperialist. He had the support not just of Conservatives but of leading Liberal politicians, too. Lord Milner, Lord Cromer and Lord Curzon not only helped to run the Empire but wrote and spoke often in its praise. Weekly magazines like the *Illustrated London News* and *The Graphic* gave plenty of coverage to imperial events, and newspapers like the *Daily Mail* and *The Times* were strongly imperialist. *The Times* was

**1 Name three leading imperialists of the 1890s.**

1 Study source 15.
  a) What does it show?
  b) What do you know about the magazine in which it was published?
  c) Would you say the artist was imperialist or anti-imperialist? Explain your answer.
2 What does the word to 'maffick' mean? Explain why this new word appeared during the South African War.

unusual for those days in having a woman colonial editor, Flora Shaw. She enjoyed the confidence of leading imperialists like Rhodes and eventually married another one, Lord Lugard. The picture 'The Gathering of the Clans' expresses the triumphant feeling that the Empire was bringing together many different nations under Britain's lead.

The middle classes were the most imperialist, but sometimes the whole nation got swept away. The Diamond Jubilee of 1897 was one moment; the relief of the town of Mafeking during the South African War in 1900 was another. On the night when the news of the relief came through, people rejoiced so riotously and extravagantly that a new word, to 'maffick', entered the English language.

15 'Sons of the Blood'. This picture of triumphant British soldiers, cheering the Union Jack on some faraway hillside, is a good example of the imperialist mood of the late nineteenth century.

# Critics of the Empire

As well as ardent supporters, the Empire had fierce critics in Britain. The huge popularity of imperialism did not prevent them from speaking out.

Many of them were members of the Liberal Party who agreed with Gladstone that imperialism, as well as being morally wrong, was likely to cause more problems than it solved. In 1879, Gladstone strongly attacked Disraeli's imperial adventures (see page 27). He told his audience that in South Africa 10,000 Zulus had been slaughtered

**16** *for no other offence than their attempt to defend against your artillery, their hearths and homes, their wives and families . . . Remember the rights of the savage! . . . Remember that the happiness of his humble home . . . is as inviolable* [sacred] *in the eye of Almighty God as can be your own.*

Quoted in James Morris, *Pax Britannica*, 1975

Another powerful Liberal critic was J. A. Hobson. He was sure that empire-building had proved bad for the business interests of the country as a whole. Huge sums of money, which would have improved the lives of most Britons if invested in home industry, had been invested much less usefully in the colonies. Why, he asked, had this happened?

**17** *Although the new Imperialism has been bad business for the nation, it has been good business for certain classes and certain trades within the nation . . . certain big firms engaged in building warships and transports . . . the great manufacturers of the export trade . . . the military services . . . the Indian Civil Service . . . and the numerous official and semi-official posts in the colonies. Every expansion of the Empire is also regarded by these same classes as affording new openings for their sons as ranchers, planters, engineers or missionaries.*

J. A. Hobson, *Imperialism, A Study*, 1902

There were also individuals who tried to stem the tide of imperialism. The poet W. S. Blunt paid for the legal defence of Colonel Arabi after his defeat and capture by British forces in 1882. Annie Besant went to India in 1893, became a Hindu, and ended up a leading figure in the Indian nationalist movement. Emily Hobhouse was a passionate opponent of the South African War who brought to public notice the treatment of Boer women and children in Kitchener's concentration camps.

3 Divide the following up into champions or critics of imperialism:
Annie Besant (page 69),
Joseph Chamberlain (page 67),
Richard Cobden (page 8),
Lord Cromer (page 34),
Benjamin Disraeli (page 11),
W. E. Gladstone (page 69),
J. A. Hobson (page 69),
Flora Shaw (page 68).

4 Why did Gladstone criticise the war against Zululand in 1878–9 (see source 16)?

5 J. A. Hobson was sure that for most Britons the Empire was 'bad business' (source 17). Who gained from it, in his opinion?

6 Popular support for the Empire declined after the South African War. Why do you think this was so?

# 7 The impact of the Empire

## Costs and benefits

In its heyday the British Empire was both loved and hated. Even today, a generation or more since it ceased to be important, it can still arouse strong feelings.

Those many Britons who helped to pay for the Victoria Memorial (source 1) really believed that the Empire was a force for good in the world. They also thought that it would last for hundreds of years. The Memorial, finished in 1921, set out to show both the strengths and the virtues of British rule. Yet by 1947, just 26 years later, India had won a bitter struggle for independence.

The Kenyans celebrating in source 2 were delighted to see the end of British rule, which, in their opinion, had done more harm than good. They, too, only won their independence after a bitter conflict during which many black and white people were killed.

After 1945, most Asians and Africans believed that the British Empire was something which the British had forced upon them against their wills, to be run at their expense in order to keep Britain rich and strong. When they achieved independence, it was their view that Britain had tried hard, though unsuccessfully, to stop them gaining their freedom.

Many Britons, by contrast, while agreeing that the Empire was mainly for Britain's benefit, thought that they had done much for their colonies. They found it hard to understand the bitter feelings of their former colonial subjects.

Communism, and especially the writings of V. I. Lenin, helped to fuel the controversy by teaching that imperialism – whether European (including British) or American – was a great evil. Many Asian and African nationalist leaders became socialists, and some became communists. Their political

**1** Statue of Edward VII and the Victoria Memorial, Calcutta.

**2**   Kenyan Independence, 1963.

parties believed that European imperialism had done great damage to their countries.

Racism added to the controversy, since white people seemed to benefit materially from the European empires while black Asian and African people suffered. Worse, many white people still thought that they deserved to benefit because they were racially superior.

Such controversies made it hard for historians to reach balanced views about the British Empire. The search for balance was made more difficult because most of the published evidence about the nineteenth-century Empire was written by Europeans, who often gave a one-sided view. Fortunately, with the passing of time, the British Empire has become less controversial and evidence provided by historians in various parts of the world has made it possible to get a more balanced view of its effects.

# The harm done by the Empire

## Costs of conquest

British conquest sometimes meant trickery and violence, leading to the theft of land and the deaths of thousands. For example, the 'pioneers' of Rhodes's British South Africa Company tricked Lobengula, the Ndebele Chief, into letting their armed column onto his land. They then seized the best land and, soon after, did the same to the neighbouring Shona people. Then, with their

1  **What is meant by 'independence'? What would have happened to British troops and civil servants in India and Kenya, once the change to independence had taken place?**

2  **What did Lenin say about European empires? (See pages 70–1.)**

3  **How did his ideas come to influence the thinking of Africans and Asians?**

4  **Explain some of the problems which historians face in writing a balanced account of the expansion of the British Empire in the late nineteenth century.**

**3** The end of the Shona rebellion of 1896.

Maxim guns and reinforcements from South Africa, they killed thousands when the Africans rose in desperate revolt. Lobengula committed suicide by taking poison.

## Land and labour

Once the British had control of the land, they took steps to make sure that the indigenous population provided cheap labour. Under no circumstances, said a British official in Kenya in 1905, will:

**4** [white people] *do manual labour in a country inhabited by black races.*

Quoted by G. H. Mungeam, *British Rule in Kenya 1895–1912*, 1966

The best way to get cheap labour was to use labour laws and tax demands to force people to stop farming their own land, which did not raise cash, and work for wages to pay their taxes. This was the method used in South Africa, for example (see pages 47–9).

## Trade

Since trade was one of the main reasons for the spread of British power across the globe, the British made sure that they controlled the most profitable trade of the Empire.

For example, George Goldie set up the Royal Niger Company in 1886. By 1895 it had used its private force of troops and ships to win a complete monopoly of the palm-oil trade of the Lower Niger. Ja-Ja, Chief of the Opobo people of the Niger delta, a clever man and successful trade, was

---

1 **What does source 3 show? Why had the Shona people risen in revolt?**

2 **Give two other examples of British cruelty while empire-building. Why was cruelty shown so frequently towards indigenous peoples?**

3 **Explain how British employers were able to get indigenous people to work for them for low wages.**

taken prisoner and removed from the area. As a British official reported back to London:

> **5** *in the vast territories of the Niger Company . . . the markets are all theirs. They can open and shut markets at will which means subsistence [just surviving] or starvation for the native inhabitants . . . they can offer any price they like to the producers, and the latter must either take it or starve.*
>
> Quoted by J. L. Flint, *Sir George Goldie and the Making of Nigeria*, 1960

The industries and crops which were developed in the colonies were those products which were most useful to the advanced economies of Britain, Europe and the USA – gold in South Africa, rubber in Malaya, cocoa in the Gold Coast, copper in Northern Rhodesia. These products were usually in the hands of businesses owned by British, European and American shareholders. Most of the profits went to the shareholders overseas – and it was in their interest to keep the wages of the indigenous workforce as low as possible. Thus the South African Chamber of Mines reported in 1902:

> **6** *the continuance and expansion of the mines, the prosperity and contentment of the white population depend . . . on an adequate supply of cheap labour through the coloured races.*
>
> Quoted in S. Marks and R. Rathbone, *Industrialisation and Social Change in South Africa*, 1982

**4** Using source 5, explain how the Royal Niger Company used its monopoly of the Niger trade. Who suffered, who gained?

**5** Using source 6, explain the importance of cheap black labour to the South African gold mines.

**7** Interior of a gold mine.

## Racial attitudes

Enormous harm was done by the racial attitudes of the majority of Britons. Inevitably, Indians were angered when, for example, an army officers' club put up this notice: 'Gentlemen are requested to refrain from [avoid] beating the natives'. The British government's policy of allowing Indian magistrates to try Europeans led to a campaign by colonial officials which revealed the full strength of their racial prejudice. A typical response came from the Englishwoman who said the policy 'would subject civilised women to the jurisdiction [judgement] of men whose social ideas are still on the verge of outer civilisation.'

## Political attitudes

Britain's double standards infuriated the colonial peoples most. Why did the British, famous throughout the world for their love of liberty and of representative government, withhold freedom and representation from their African and Asian colonies? Why did they imprison or drive into exile leaders like Colonel Arabi in Egypt, or Tilak in India, or Cetshwayo in South Africa, or Ja-Ja in Nigeria who were only trying to win rights which they knew should be theirs?

8 The trial of Colonel Arabi, captured by an *Illustrated London News* artist, 23 December 1882.

# The benefits of British rule to the colonies

The main benefits came from two important causes of British expansion: the advanced nature of British technology, and the determination of many Britons to bring about genuine humanitarian improvements.

## Technological improvements

British engineering skills meant better roads, railways, steamboats and irrigation schemes. Roads like those from the Gold Coast ports into the interior, for example, or railways like those from Cape Town to Salisbury, opened up vast areas to greater trade and wider human contact. When the Uganda railway from the Kenyan port of Mombasa finally reached Lake Victoria, a steamboat was there to meet it. This vessel had been prefabricated in England and carried in hundreds of pieces overland to the lakeshore, where it had been reassembled.

**9  A railway bridge built in 1900 near Quetta, now in modern Pakistan.**

In India, 40,000 miles of canal were built, irrigating 20 million acres. Near Bombay was the Tansa dam, two miles long and 35 metres high, at that time one of the largest constructions in the world. These improvements offered some protection against the terrible famines which struck the Indian subcontinent from time to time.

## Peace and order

Though they were often ruthless when imposing or asserting their control, the British attempted to rule fairly and keep the Empire at peace. They ended the slave trade which had caused so much misery in Central Africa and outlawed practices such as *suttee*, which required widows in parts of India to be burnt to death on the funeral pyres of their husbands. Many of the areas they conquered had suffered from frequent wars in the past: the Pax Britannica or British Peace was often a genuine achievement as well as a source of great pride.

**4  What does the phrase 'Pax Britannica' mean?**

1  List eight good things which the
   Empire brought to its subjects.
2  Which do you consider the
   most important as far as the
   welfare of the subject peoples
   was concerned?

## Humanitarian improvements

Along with more functional improvements, such as better railways and roads, and the stability of the Pax Britannica, came social and humanitarian improvements like education and hospitals, banks and post offices, newspapers and magazines. Outstanding contributions were often made by individuals in these areas. For example, Elizabeth Bielby, who came out to India as a medical missionary, trained as a doctor and founded a woman's hospital in Lahore which she ran from 1888 to 1903.

**10**  A hospital.

## Introducing new (Western) ideas

The Christian missions, the schools and the universities introduced Africans and Asians to British, European and American (Western) ideas about all sorts of things, politics included. Some of the founders of the South African Native National Congress had started their education in Christian mission schools and completed it in American colleges. Gandhi, the leader of the Indian independence movement after the First World War, trained as a lawyer in London while Nehru, India's first Prime Minister, was educated at Harrow and Cambridge. They learnt the value of freedom, representative government, social justice and national unity. When eventually they led their nations to freedom and independence, it was not back to the ways of the old pre-British days but to new societies where non-Western ideas mingled with Western ones.

However, whatever benefits the Empire may have brought to the colonies, they were given by free rulers to unfree subjects. For that important reason they were less appreciated. As the Egyptian nationalist, Mustafa Kamil, eloquently explained in a letter to the British Prime Minister, Campbell-Bannerman (a Liberal) in 1907:

> **11** *There is no level of prosperity that can make a man set aside his dignity, his mission in life, the freedom of his country . . . the chains of slavery are still chains whether they be forged of gold or of iron.*
>
> Quoted by Lutfi al-Sayyid, *Egypt and Cromer*, 1968

# The benefits which the Empire brought to Britain

Britain was the most powerful nation in the world between 1815 and 1870. From then on, she was struggling to hold her own, first against the USA and Germany, then against the USSR, Japan and her neighbours in Europe. As we have seen, the main reason why the British government increased the size of the British Empire after 1870 was to defend the economic and imperial position which Britain already occupied.

## Economic benefits

There seems little doubt that the British Empire helped Britain stay rich and grow richer well into the twentieth century. British businesses and their shareholders did well out of the South African goldfields, the Malayan rubber plantations and other such investments (though Rhodes's British South African Company in Rhodesia never paid its shareholders anything at all). British companies sold large amounts in imperial markets, particularly the Lancashire cotton manufacturers. To get the Indians to pay for the Indian army and then use that army all over the Empire was great value for money, as far as the British taxpayer was concerned.

3 Give three examples of how Britain benefited economically from the Empire.
4 Give two examples of the strategic benefits which the Empire brought to Britain.

## Strategic benefits

On the whole, British politicians played their cards well between 1870 and 1914. They kept the French out of Egypt and the Sudan, Germany away from the gold mines of South Africa, Russia from the borders of India. If all their imperial rivals gained some land, the British gained much more. At the same time, they kept the support of the settler dominions so that in each of the World Wars Canadians, Australians, New Zealanders and South Africans fought beside the British, who could also rely on the troops of the large Indian army.

1 **Why, in 1935, did Winston Churchill strongly oppose the government's policy of giving India more self-government?**

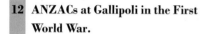

12 **ANZACs at Gallipoli in the First World War.**

From 1870 to 1945, Britain with its Empire managed to give the impression that it was a world power, alongside the USA, Germany and Russia. In 1935, the British House of Commons discussed giving self-government to India. Winston Churchill strongly attacked the idea. Self-government would quickly lead to an independent India and, without India, the British Empire would collapse. Without the Empire, Britain would immediately slip from a first-class to a third-rate power. Although in the Second World War Britain was still seen as one of the major powers, this is very much what happened after the War, between 1947 and 1980.

13 **Churchill, one of the Big Three, with Roosevelt and Stalin at Yalta in 1945.**

# The harm caused to Britain by the Empire

### Facing realities?

Some politicians, economists and historians argue that the Empire shielded the British for a century from realities they should have faced in 1870. By that date, some British industries and businesses had difficulty in competing directly with European and American rivals. Perhaps money that was being invested in the colonies should have been used to strengthen Britain's economy at home. The additional imperial trade from 1870 to 1945 meant that getting to grips with these problems was postponed. As time passed, they became harder to solve.

The Empire, holding together until the loss of India in 1947, looked so good on maps that it gave Britons a false sense of their country's strength. Most were very cool in the 1950s about the moves towards European unity. With the British Empire turning into the Commonwealth of independent but still apparently friendly ex-colonies, why should Britain bother?

However, when the European Community flourished and the Commonwealth turned out to be little more than an international club for countries with historic and cultural links, this coolness was seen by many to have been a mistake. In 1962, Dean Acheson, Secretary of State, remarked that:

**14** *Great Britain has lost an Empire but not yet found a role.*

Quoted by K. Robbins, *The Eclipse of a Great Power*, 1983

What Acheson meant was that the British Empire had made Britons confident of their world position, but without it they had no sense of where they stood in a rapidly changing world.

**15** Cartoon of Empire.

# Conclusion

At the height of the Diamond Jubilee celebrations in 1897, when the Empire seemed at its strongest and most confident, Rudyard Kipling's poem 'Recessional' warned of a time when it would all be gone:

**16** *Far-called, our navies melt away;*
*On dune and headland sinks the fire;*
*Lo, all our pomp of yesterday,*
*Is one with Nineveh and Tyre!*
*Judge of the Nations, spare us yet,*
*Lest we forget – lest we forget!*

Rudyard Kipling, 'Recessional', 1897

Few then realised that it would fade so soon, but in reality Britain's real power in comparison with other nations was already on the wane.

**17** *The real significance of the Empire almost all along had been simply that it cushioned [Britain's] fall in the world. From 1870 to 1980 and possibly beyond, the history of Britain has been one of steady and almost unbroken decline, economically, militarily, and politically relative to other nations ... What the Empire did do was to shield Britain against some of the consequences, and especially the economic consequences of decline, like layers of warm clothing round an ailing body ...*

Bernard Porter, *The Lion's Share*, 1984

2 Many historians believe that the Empire allowed Britain to avoid facing a serious problem which had started as early as 1870. What problem was that?

3 What was Dean Acheson getting at in 1962 (source 14)?

4 Explain the cartoon in source 15.

5 What do you see as a sensible role for Britain in the twenty-first century?

6 Bernard Porter (source 17) describes the British Empire as a 'cushion' or as a 'layer of warm clothing'. Do you think that, in the long run, it was a good thing
a) for Britain,
b) for the rest of the world?
Explain your answers.

George Bernard Shaw, political writer and playwright:

> **1** *When he* [the Englishman] *wants a new market for his adulterated* [poor quality] *Manchester goods, he sends a missionary to teach the Gospel of Peace. The natives kill the missionary; he flies to arms in defence of Christianity; conquers for it and takes the market as a reward from heaven.*

**1** Re-read pages 58 and 59
Explain the stages by which, according to Source 1 (above), missionaries helped the English expand their trade all over the world. Do you think this source gives a fair view of missionary activity?

Jawahadel Nehru, writing in 1946 about British rule:

> **2** *It is difficult to say what Indians have resented* [disliked] *most in the record of British rule . . . India had to bear the cost of her own conquest . . . and for expeditions to Africa, Persia etc . . . the lack of industry and the neglect of agriculture . . . the extreme backwardness of the social services; and above all the tragic poverty of the country.*

**2** Who was Nehru? How valuable are his comments about the effect of the British Empire on India?

**3** How did India bear the cost of expeditions to Africa?

**4** Re-read pages 75 and 76. How might a British civil servant who had devoted his working life to India have answered Nehru's criticisms?

**5** Reviewing the British Empire between 1870 and 1914, write an essay with three parts:
  **a** How did the Empire affect the colonies?
  **b** How did it effect Britain?
  **c** Did it do more good than harm?